PLANTING DESIGNS FOR
CACTUS &
SUCCULENTS

INDOOR & OUTDOOR PROJECTS FOR UNIQUE, EASY-CARE PLANTS—IN ALL CLIMATES

SHARON ASAKAWA AND JOHN BAGNASCO

with

SHAUN BUCHANAN, PHOTOGRAPHER

and

ROBYN FOREMAN, PROJECT DESIGNER

COOL
SPRINGS
PRESS
Home and Garden Experts™

MINNEAPOLIS, MINNESOTA

First published in 2013 by Cool Springs Press, an imprint of the Quayside Publishing Group, 400 First Avenue North, Suite 400, Minneapolis, MN 55401

© 2013 Cool Springs Press
Text © Sharon Asakawa and John Bagnasco 2013
Photos © Shaun Buchanan 2013
Project designs by Robyn Foreman 2013

Cool Springs Press titles are also available at discounts in bulk quantity for industrial or sales-promotional use. For details write to Special Sales Manager at Cool Springs Press, 400 First Avenue North, Suite 400, Minneapolis, MN 55401 USA. To find out more about our books, visit us online at www.coolspringspress.com.

ISBN: 978-1-59186-561-2

Library of Congress Cataloging-in-Publication Data

Asakawa, Sharon.
  Planting designs for cactus & succulents : indoor & outdoor uses for unique, easy-care plants-in all climates / Sharon Asakawa and John Bagnasco ; with Shaun Buchanan, photographer and Robyn Foreman, project designer.
    p. cm.
  Planting designs for cactus and succulents
  Includes index.
  ISBN 978-1-59186-561-2 (sc)
  1. Cactus. 2. Succulent plants. I. Bagnasco, John. II. Buchanan, Shaun. III. Foreman, Robyn. IV. Title. V. Title: Planting designs for cactus and succulents.

  SB438.A72 2014
  634'.775--dc23
                                2013036438

Acquisitions Editor: Billie Brownell
Design Manager: Cindy Samargia Laun
Design: Simon Larkin
Layout: Erin Fahringer
Cover Design: Michelle Thompson

Printed in China
10 9 8 7 6 5 4 3 2 1

Additional Credits
For page 79, Bridal Bouquet:
Hair and Makeup by Melissa Rae & Co.,
www.MelissaRaeMakeup.com

For page 105, Raise the Wroof:
Doghouse courtesy of "Doggy Den" provided by PetSqueak.
www.PetSqueak.com.
Photo star: "Pete" the Australian shepherd.

For page 139, Wine Bottle Cork Rest:
Photos taken inside Witch Creek Winery, Carlsbad, California

PLANTING DESIGNS FOR

CACTUS &
SUCCULENTS

INDOOR & OUTDOOR PROJECTS FOR UNIQUE, EASY-CARE PLANTS—IN ALL CLIMATES

SHARON ASAKAWA AND JOHN BAGNASCO

with

SHAUN BUCHANAN, PHOTOGRAPHER

and

ROBYN FOREMAN, PROJECT DESIGNER

DEDICATION

To all the enthusiasts of weirdly wonderful succulent plants around the globe.

For Bruce, the kindest and most loving husband who shared all his horticultural teachable moments with me, and for our children and their families: Eric, Stephanie, and Samokai; and Tasia, Claudio, Nicholas, and Emiko. May the family tree continue to grow and flourish.

—Sharon

For my beautiful, wise, and loving wife Shannon, who has put up with my plant "addiction" for over forty years. And for our children and their spouses, Joe and Shanell; Gina and Sam; and Jesse and Andy. Also, to our granddaughter Kendyl Marie, who is being raised with laughter, adventure, and discovery.

—John

If it were not for the extensive patience, loving support, and sheer brute strength of my husband Jeff and my two cooperative, fun-loving kids, Heather and Todd, none of these designs could have been developed and made it to the page. Thank you for your love, help, and input and for putting up with countless weekends without your wife and mother. Thanks for accepting me as I am, soil packed fingernails and all. I adore you.

—Robyn

For the love of my life, my wife Kathryn Buchanan. She put up with me being gone every weekend to shoot pictures all over Southern California and supported me through the whole project. Also, to my parents, Pamela and Richard Buchanan, and my sister and her husband, Brittany and Matthew Herbison, for supporting me and driving me to seek a creative path through life. For this, I love you all.

—Shaun

ACKNOWLEDGMENTS

We owe the completion of this project to many of our gardening friends and peers. In today's busy world, people are often reluctant to take time out of their swamped schedules for projects in which they are not directly involved. We are grateful to each and every person who made this book possible. As for the authors, this work was a true collaboration, and it really helped that the four of us actually like one another!

The authors would like to express a sincere thanks to Ken and Deena Altman whose decades of devotion to succulent propagation have made these wonderful plants more readily available to the general public. We appreciate the resources they allowed us to use in the preparation of all the design projects. We would also like to note our gratitude to Carmen Conteras at Oasis Water Efficient Gardens in Escondido, California. Her enthusiasm for succulent plants is both boundless and contagious.

For supporting us during this project, we'd like to acknowledge all of our friends and relatives including, but not limited to, Bruce Asakawa, Shannon Bagnasco, Kathryn Buchanan, Heather Foreman, Jeff Foreman, Todd Foreman, Janet Gauger, Stewart Gauger, and Bob Reidmuller. We would also like to thank our garden writer friends, such as Debra Lee Baldwin, for continuing to popularize this unique group of plants through books that are so well received by the public.

And thanks to Tracy Stanley and all the amazing people at the Quayside Publishing Group for the opportunity to work on this venture, with a special thanks to our editor, Billie Brownell, whose guidance, support, and direction really made this book possible. We are pleased and proud to have our book published by such a fine press.

CONTENTS

19 LANDSCAPE ACCENTS

63 INTERIOR ACCENTS

77 WEDDINGS, PARTIES, AND SPECIAL EVENTS

105 RAISE THE WROOF!

113 KID-FRIENDLY PROJECTS

123 BACK-TO-NATURE PROJECTS

141 SEASONAL ARRANGEMENTS

151 OUTDOOR DÉCOR PROJECTS

161 BASICS OF SUCCULENT CARE

166 BASICS OF SUCCULENT PROPAGATION

INTRODUCTION

If plants governed the natural world, succulents would definitely be placed along the conservative spectrum and cacti would align themselves even farther along at the end, considering themselves among the ultra conservative group. Together they subscribe to the thrifty philosophy of water use as opposed to those at the opposite end of the spectrum, their more liberal brethren, the thirsty ferns and tropicals that imbibe as if there were no "moisture ceiling." However, just as no single set of ideologies is universally regarded as conservative versus liberal, so it is with succulents in the plant kingdom. There is no categorical definition of a succulent, and as in the political spectrum, there are varying degrees of "succulence," with many plants being marginally so.

Because they are beautiful, unique, and nearly indestructible if not overwatered, cacti and succulents are gaining in popularity with gardeners, homeowners, and hobbyists. Scientifically, a succulent plant is one that has fat leaves, stems, or roots containing water storage organs. These organs allow the plants to adapt and to

survive harsh, arid climates throughout the world. The best part about this survival mechanism for gardeners is that in many cases the plants have developed into an eye-popping assortment of alluring leaf forms and plant shapes.

As a coterie, succulents include some of the world's best-loved classes of flora, such as aloe, agave, echeveria, and euphorbia, along with a host of exotic curiosities as well as blooming accents whether placed directly in the landscape or in containers. Cacti, which are endemic to only the new world, are a specific order of the succulent group that are distinguished by having spines emanating from specialized structures known as areoles. This is why those in the know trot out the quote, "All cacti are succulents, but not all succulents are cacti."

The purpose of this book is not to reconstruct the body of literature that so many experts have already ably researched and offered. Rather, it is meant to be an illumination into the extreme resilience of this matchless group of plants and to facilitate some fun ideas for projects that are truly

remarkable yet easily replicated for indoors and outdoors. Hopefully, it will become evident that no matter what type of succulents are chosen for a project, a governing body of rules for their care and propagation will generally apply (see the section on Basics of Succulent Care on pg. 160).

Projects in this book embody simple design principles. Color coordination, step-by-step instructions on how to create container gardens, doorways, and step pavers made out of succulents, and fascinating xerispheres are just a few of the concepts covered. From the voguish bouquets for weddings, parties, and special events to kid-friendly designs and even the environmentally friendly green roofs for birdhouses and doghouses, there is an activity that will intrigue novices and green thumbs alike. Imagination is the only constraint to the wondrous world of succulents.

As Google Maps provides directions to both dramatic and commonplace sites around the globe, this work is intended to guide the reader through the enchanting universe from workhorse succulents in

Garden Door, page 39

Life Is A Ball, page 101

the landscape to specimen standouts, prized bloomers, and those that are weirdly wonderful. Succulent plants are also very forgiving and extremely low maintenance, so take a leap of faith, choose the path without a road sign, and be prepared to find something amazing and serendipitous along the way. Discover how much fun it is to create a clever, easy-to-care-for container or landscape accent using some truly remarkable plants.

While cacti and succulents have captivated the botanical community for several centuries, their versatility has now placed them in the pantheon of plant trendiness for the twenty-first century. Whether the preference is for structural form and Zen simplicity, a carnival of riotous color, or a hauntingly odd appearance, there is a place for every taste, and the following projects will illustrate how to highlight them in all their unique glory. Once begun, it will be easy and more fun to follow the path of the conservative plant world rather than the more liberal and high-maintenance water guzzlers.

Succulent "Grout" for Steppingstones, page 31

Dry Bottle Gardens, page 137

Living Stones, page 131

Buoyant Enchantment, page 97

A Living Succulent Table, page 155

Falling for Autumn, page 146

Raise the Wroof, page 105

Clay Dish Garden, page 75

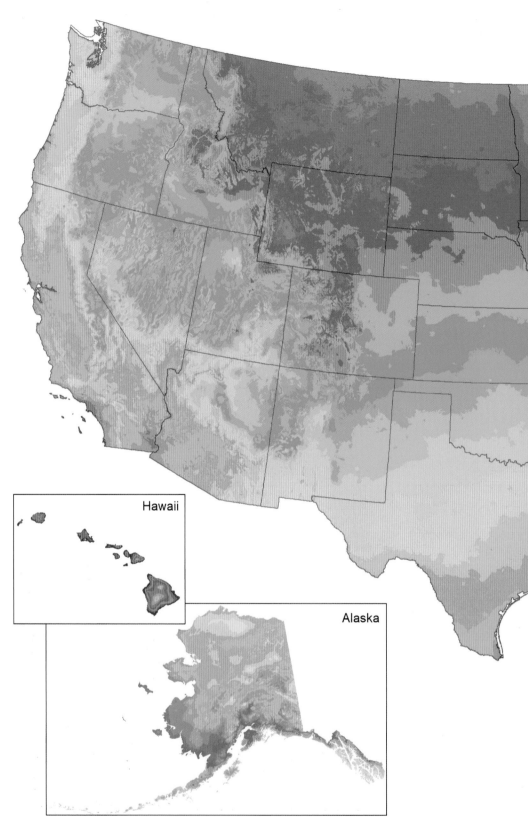

Hawaii

Alaska

USDA Plant Hardiness Zone Map, 2012. Agricultural Research Service, U.S. Department of Agriculture. Accessed from http://planthardiness.ars.usda.gov.

USDA Plant Hardiness Zone Map

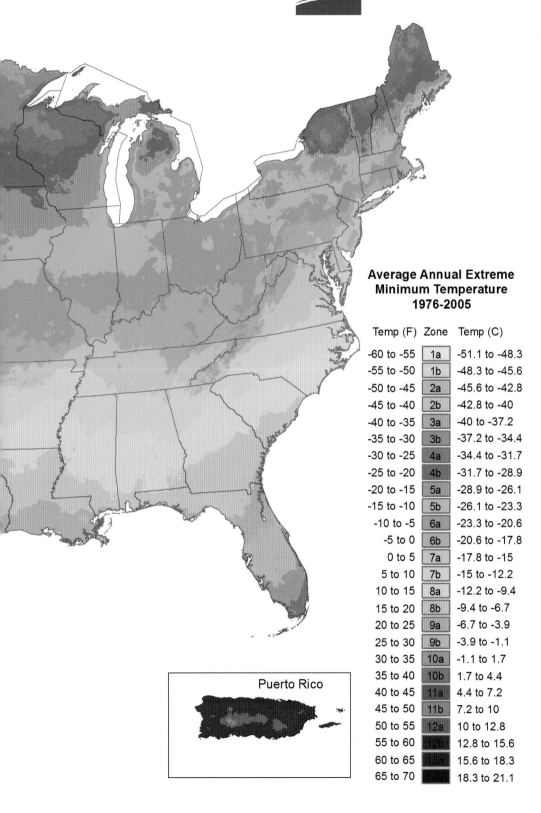

Average Annual Extreme Minimum Temperature 1976-2005

Temp (F)	Zone	Temp (C)
-60 to -55	1a	-51.1 to -48.3
-55 to -50	1b	-48.3 to -45.6
-50 to -45	2a	-45.6 to -42.8
-45 to -40	2b	-42.8 to -40
-40 to -35	3a	-40 to -37.2
-35 to -30	3b	-37.2 to -34.4
-30 to -25	4a	-34.4 to -31.7
-25 to -20	4b	-31.7 to -28.9
-20 to -15	5a	-28.9 to -26.1
-15 to -10	5b	-26.1 to -23.3
-10 to -5	6a	-23.3 to -20.6
-5 to 0	6b	-20.6 to -17.8
0 to 5	7a	-17.8 to -15
5 to 10	7b	-15 to -12.2
10 to 15	8a	-12.2 to -9.4
15 to 20	8b	-9.4 to -6.7
20 to 25	9a	-6.7 to -3.9
25 to 30	9b	-3.9 to -1.1
30 to 35	10a	-1.1 to 1.7
35 to 40	10b	1.7 to 4.4
40 to 45	11a	4.4 to 7.2
45 to 50	11b	7.2 to 10
50 to 55	12a	10 to 12.8
55 to 60	12b	12.8 to 15.6
60 to 65	13a	15.6 to 18.3
65 to 70		18.3 to 21.1

Puerto Rico

LANDSCAPE ACCENTS

Plants armed with razor-sharp spines or swollen, fleshy, moisture-retentive leaves and branches. What's the allure? Why would an encounter with blood-drawing spines or plants described as "thick and fleshy" encourage gardeners to use them in the landscape? Perhaps the irresistible draw is that they are so extraordinarily different from other plants in the temperate world. One of the first plants brought back by explorers from the New World was the *Opuntia*, commonly called the cactus fig plant, known for its edible prickly pear fruit and nopales pads and also carmine dyes made from the cochineal scale found on opuntia. By the eighteenth century, the dye was so popular in Europe that it was listed on the commodity exchanges of London and Amsterdam. Soon bold *Agave* species became the plant rock stars in Europe, and Victorians coveted cactus such as *Echinocactus*, known as fat plants or curiosity plants.

For many parts of the country, it is possible to incorporate these unique and water-thrifty plants either directly in the landscape or in containers large and small. Although there are gorgeous flowering cactus and succulents, the most stunning attribute is their sculptural or branching structures, dominating the landscape with spirals, mounds, and whorls, lifting eyes skyward. Trees are visual screens, while cactus and succulents lend themselves to the principles of open space and transparency. Think of the vast sparseness of their native habitat. The desert, for example, is the ultimate minimalist landscape. Likewise, in the home landscape, if space is allowed, each specimen should be given its proper attention.

Rather than an extensive treatise on landscape principles for the water-thrifty garden, this chapter is more about how succulents can contribute to the decorative art of gardens and to encourage readers to "just do it" with simple but inspiring ideas. It is meant to encourage all to go forth where no timid gardener has gone before and adapt the "anything goes" philosophy by using bright, colorful walls; small-scale, make-it-yourself hypertufa trough containers; even recycled materials such as an old door or broken pavers to show off a "grout" composed of clusters of succulents.

Many succulents such as *Aeonium* are rosettes, bunching their green, purplish black, or rainbow-colored variegated leaves on short stems and are ideal for massing in borders, containers, or rock gardens. *Sedums* and ice plants are reliable, verdant carpets for the ground or beyond, ideal for tumbling over hanging baskets, but in spring, they suddenly burst forth with sparkling pink, magenta, apricot, and other colors of the rainbow, smothering their foliar mats with flowers. The sharp tips of *Agave* plants or the pointed spines of cactus make protective borders against unwanted intruders. *Echeveria* with their vibrant colors and spectacular rosettes are particularly vivid in the cooler months, while *Crassula* species, with their moisture-holding leaves planted around homes, rocky embankments, or slopes, provide a fire-retardant barrier.

Some of the most bodacious flowers announce their arrival on even the humblest of cactus, transforming a stand of *Opuntia* into exotic flower factories. Or how about a dramatic grouping of golden barrel cactus to trick the eye into seeing rolling hills planted near the "peaks" of densely white-hair-covered columns of old man of the Andes and color contrasting with the powdery blue *Agave* 'Boutin Blue'? If certain succulent or cactus varieties are frost tender, select others that survive in zones 5–6, such as many *Sedum*, *Crassula*, and ice plants, or push the zonal envelope and plant varieties in containers to move indoors during seasons of inclement weather. Whether the preference is for the more common *Sempervivum* species such as hens and chicks or for the show-stopping "what is that?" such as the tree aloe, cow horn plant, or Eve's needle cactus, adding a few to the home landscape may be the beginning of a beautiful friendship.

SUCCULENTS AND CACTI

AEONIUM

Most *Aeonium* species are from the Canary Islands and have stunning rosettes of distinctive leaf colors and textures. The rosettes emerge on the ends of branches, and the color choices, oh my! From burgundy-black to rose, bright green and yellow, and a myriad of variegations, the spoon-shaped leafy rosettes bear conical stalks of petite, primarily yellow flowers (although some species and hybrids offer other floral hues) in the spring or summer. The branch is monocarpic, meaning once it flowers, the branch will die, but *Aeonium* form offsets freely. Being cool-season growers, they are dormant during the summer months but will revive and grow when cooler temperatures return. Although the majority of *Aeonium* species are hardy down to 25–30°F, they may suffer from frost damage. For planting techniques and care information, see pgs. 158–163.

Common Name/Botanical Name
Aeonium
Aeonium spp.

Botanical Pronunciation
EYE-own-ee-um

LANDSCAPING TIPS & IDEAS

Low-growing, mounded *Aeonium* plants are decorative in rock gardens, combined with other succulents in containers, or in front of borders.

ALL ABOUT

The hybrid 'Kiwi' foliage has yellow centers that progressively transition from lime green to pink, edged in red, growing 2–3 ft. x as wide, bearing yellow flowers in the summer. *A. arboreum* 'Zwartkop' is prized for its dark, purplish black rosettes with chartreuse centers and grows 3–4 ft. x 1–2 ft.; in summer, large clusters of yellow flowers emerge from its center. *A. tabuliforme*, or saucer plant, is composed of a mass of hairy, fleshy, green leaves that form flat rosettes like a dinner plate measuring 2 in. x 8 in. *A. arboreum*, different from varieties such as 'Zwartkop' and 'Atropurpureum', with waxy sprightly green foliage measuring 1–3 ft. x 3 ft. and bearing stunning pyramidal panicles of yellow flowers in spring. *A. canariense* is a species that may have either smooth or fuzzy pale green leaves depending on the variety, forming a dense, swirling, slow-growing rosette measuring 1 ft. x 2–3 ft. and bearing pale green to white flowers in winter or spring. As the leaves age, their color will fade to a pinkish red at the ends.

AGAVE

Most *Agave* species come from Mexico or the Southwest and include fibrous-leaved specimens, often with stiff leaves tipped with sharp points. Whether upright in habit, such as the tequila agave, or spherical, such as the hedgehog agave, these monocarpic plants all make bold, architectural statements in the landscape but should be planted away from pathways for safety. Wear thick, protective gloves whenever handling due to their irritating sap, sharp tips, and thorns. Although most are hardy down to 25–30°F, there may be frost damage. For planting techniques and care information, see pgs. 160-165.

LANDSCAPING TIPS & IDEAS

Use agaves as single specimen focal points in the landscape or containers or in rock gardens with other succulents, but keep armored varieties away from paths or play areas. Plant the spiral-form Queen Victoria in a wide, shallow container to show off its beauty when viewed from above.

ALL ABOUT

'Boutin Blue' has broad, powdery blue leaves with no spikes, 3–4 ft. x as wide. *A. stricta*, 2 ft. x 2 ft. with narrow foliage and spiny tips, grows into a spherical shape and bears reddish purple flowers on 6 ft. stems in summer. *A. victoriae-reginae* bears distinctive single rosettes 12–15 in. across with deep green, stiff, thick, blunt-shaped 6 in. leaves with thin white margins and sharp black terminal spines; may take years to blossom. The monocarpic *A. americana* 'Variegata', 3–4 ft. x as wide with broad bold yellow or white striped leaves and poisonous sharp spines that can be cut off for safety; after 8–10 years, its fast-growing flower stalk (6–14 in. per day) resembles a giant asparagus until the greenish yellow flowers appear. *A. tequilana* is the fast-growing, 4–6 ft. x as wide plant used to make tequila. It has 7-ft.-long blue-gray leaves with sharp spines and teeth along the margins. *A. vilmoriniana* is called the octopus agave because of its thin, spineless green leaves that twist and turn, resembling tentacles. If planted on slopes, they look like giant spiders on a wall.

ALOE

Primarily from South Africa, *Aloe* species are bold perennials that range in size from elfin 6 in. varieties to statuesque trees with green or grayish green leaves arranged in rosettes or spirals in clumping, sprawling, or semiclimbing habits. Although some are edged with teeth, most are not as sharp or thorny as *Agave*. Depending on the species, there are *Aloe* that bloom every month of the year, but the most common floral flourishes occur in midwinter to summer in a variety of colors, and leaves also come banded or streaked in contrasting hues. For planting techniques and care information, see pgs. 160-165.

LANDSCAPING TIPS & IDEAS

Popular for dry landscapes or pollinator-friendly gardens in Mediterranean climates, use the *A. ferox* species with its 8–10 ft.-tall trunk topped with a rosette of 3–4 ft.-wide leaves as a focal point, or plant a mass of *A. aculeata* with their orange to yellow spikes of poker-shaped flower clusters. For rock gardens, *A. petricola* thrives among stones. In colder zones, plant aloes in containers so they can be moved during inclement weather.

ALL ABOUT

A. aculeata, whose common name is red hot poker, is stemless with sharp white bumps along the leaves, growing 2 ft. x 3 ft. From dense foliar rosettes, orange-blending-to-yellow spikes of flowers appear in winter/spring. In late autumn/early winter, the *A. ferox* species bears hundreds of red or orange blossoms on candelabra-shaped heads; however, 'Sophie' is more petite, growing 6–12 in., and its yellow flowering spikes bloom from early spring to fall. *A. ciliaris*, a.k.a. the climbing aloe because of its fast-growing, 8–12 ft. x spreading habit. It has thin, green stems edged with teeth bearing green or yellow-tipped, reddish orange flowers that bloom periodically throughout the year. *A. petricola* is native to the rocky slopes of South Africa and is a stemless aloe, 18–24 in. x 2–3 ft., with broad blue-gray leaves that curl into a ball-like form. In winter, bicolored creamy yellow flowers emerge. *A. vera*, valued as a medicinal burn emollient, has upright, 1–2 ft. tall leaves with yellow flowers blooming in spring and summer.

Common Name/Botanical Name
Aloe
Aloe spp.

Botanical Pronunciation
a-LOE

CACTUS

Most cacti are endemic to the Americas and have modified, water-storing stems that are jointed, pad-shaped, or cylindrical instead of leaves. They also have wicked spines to ward off browsing animals and human handlers, but compensate with brilliant flowers that hold their own against the flashiest garden variety plants and that are hummingbird magnets. A stand of *Opuntia* transforms its pads into eye-candy flower factories followed by red fruit, barrel cactus produces lovely flowers crowning its tops, and old man of the Andes bears red tubular flowers. If there are suitable spots for prickly plants, cacti provide structure, texture, and color to the dry landscape. For planting techniques and care information, see pgs. 160-165.

LANDSCAPING TIPS & IDEAS

Take advantage of their clustering habit and plant golden barrel cactus (*Echinocactus grussonii*) *en masse* to fool the eye into seeing rolling hills. Pop the landscape with the white-haired old man of the Andes (*Orocereus celsianus*). Where winter freezes are common, plant in containers, especially the smaller San Diego barrel cactus (*Ferocactus viridescens*) or twin-spined cactus (*Mammillaria geminispina*).

ALL ABOUT

Golden barrel cactus (*Echinocactus grussonii*) has yellow spines along its ribs, producing offsets that form 6-ft.-wide rounded clumps (takes years to bloom). Wheel cactus, or silver dollar prickly pear (*Opuntia robusta*), has multiple-branched, bluish green stems that are flattened, somewhat circular, and covered in spines and raised bumps resembling small bristles with spring flowers followed by fruit. Old man of the Andes (*Orocereus celsianus*) is a white-hair-covered columnar cactus standing 10 ft. with brown spines and red tubular flowers in spring. Silver or woolly torch (*Cleistocactus strausii*) has cylindrical, 8–10 ft. columns covered with silvery white spines and burgundy-red flowers that protrude horizontally in summer. Coastal or San Diego barrel cactus (*Ferocactus viridescens*) is cylindrical when mature (usually wider than its 12 in. height) with spine-covered ribs and yellowish flowers followed by fruit. Twin-spined cactus (*Mammillaria geminispina*) forms spherical 2–3 ft. mounds composed of green stems covered in white down and white spines with magenta flowers in spring or fall.

Common Name/Botanical Name
Cactus
Various genera

Common Name/Botanical Name
Crassula
Crassula gollum

Botanical Pronunciation
KRASS-you-lah

Common Name/Botanical Name
Echeveria
Echeveria cameo

Botanical Pronunciation
Ech-eh-VER-ee-a

CRASSULA AND ECHEVERIA

The *Crassula* genus is composed of a large number of species, including the ever-popular jade plant, *C. ovata*, found throughout the world, but most cultivars come from South Africa or Madagascar. They not only vary in shape and color, but also range in size from tiny specimens to large shrubs. *Echeveria* is native primarily to Mexico and Central America, and succulent collectors covet them for their beauty and variety. Their colors are most brilliant during winter. For planting techniques and care information, see pgs. 160-165.

LANDSCAPING TIPS & IDEAS

C. arborescens looks great on slopes, rock gardens, or in containers as a silvery-colored contrast with green-leafed succulents such as *C. ovata* 'Gollum'. Where summers are mild, *Echeveria* hybrids such as 'Afterglow', 'Perle Von Nurnberg', and 'Topsy Turvy' add color and texture to dry beds or when planted with sedums in borders. Echeverias can also grow indoors where there is bright, indirect light. All are hardy down to 25–30°F except the airplane or propeller plant.

ALL ABOUT

C. falcata, known as airplane or propeller plant (2–3 ft. x as wide), has overlapping pairs of gray-green, incurved leaves resembling airplane wings and bears petite, scarlet-red flowers in summer. *Echeveria* 'Perle Von Nurnberg' has 5–6 in. rosettes of lavender-blue foliage lightly overcast in powdery white and coral flowers with yellow interiors appearing in summer. *Echeveria* 'Topsy Turvy' (12 in. x as wide) forms rosettes of thick, silvery blue leaves that are curved upward and inward and in late summer/fall bears orange and yellow flowers. *C. arborescens*, common name silver jade or silver dollar plant (4–5 ft. x as wide), is slow growing with thick branches of silvery green, fleshy leaves edged and dotted in maroon-red and bears star-shaped pinkish white flowers in spring. *C. ovata* 'Gollum' (2–3 ft. x 1–2 ft.) resembles its J. R. R. Tolkien's namesake because of its small stature and tubular leaves with suction-cup-like tips. *Echeveria* 'Afterglow' (1–2 ft. x as wide) has rosettes of pink-edged, tapered leaves that seem dusted with powdery pinkish lavender colors, giving it a glowing appearance.

GROUNDCOVERS

Think of a succulent groundcover as a textural carpet, but it also typically grows quickly, chokes out weeds, retains moisture, and serves as a fire-retardant barrier. Additionally, most succulent groundcovers such as ice plant suddenly bloom in luminescent shades of yellow, magenta, apricot, red, or white. Their foliage and flowers provide a vital landscape dimension by drawing the eye downward and livening up an otherwise drab earth. For planting techniques and care information, see pgs. 160-165.

LANDSCAPING TIPS & IDEAS

Birds, bees, and butterflies linger and flit over succulent groundcovers when in bloom, but the following succulents can also cover slopes, particularly south-facing inclines; fill in rock gardens; cascade down walls; or create borders. In the past, *Sempervivum tectorum* (hens and chicks) were called houseleeks because they were planted on roofs in the belief that they protected against lightning. Although rooftops remain popular spots to plant succulent groundcovers today, the purpose is for insulation, water conservation, and beauty. Where winter frost is common, *Sedum lucidum*, *Sempervivum tectorum*, and *Senecio scaposus* do well in moveable hanging baskets or specimen planters.

ALL ABOUT

Mesembryanthemum and *Delosperma* (1–3 in. x 8–36 in.) are two genera known as ice plants that bear white, pink, yellow, purple, red, magenta, and salmon flowers atop fleshy leaves. From South Africa, they are among the most popular groundcovers. *Sedum lucidum* (6–12 in. x as wide) is from Mexico, grows in poor soil and on rock walls, bearing sprays of yellow-eyed white flowers in spring over rounded, green leaves edged in red. *Sempervivum tectorum* (2–5 in. x 2 ft.) is commonly known as hens and chicks, and native to the mountains of southern Europe; it has different-colored rosette foliage, depending on the cultivar, and bristly reddish brown tips. Once the mother rosette (hen) blooms (reddish brown) in summer and produces offsets, it will die. *Senecio scaposus* (1 ft. x as wide), a South African native that forms cobweb-shaped rosettes of silvery, banana-shaped leaves that angle upward in tufts and bears flowers resembling coral-yellow daisies in summer.

Common Name/Botanical Name
Groundcovers
Various genera

SPECIMEN PLANTS

Several striking succulents have their place as specimen plants used to spotlight an "ooh and ah" section of the garden or home. *Aloe dichotoma* with its stocky trunk and rounded form, *Euphorbia ammak* with its candelabra-shaped top, or *Euphorbia grandicommis* with its angular stems do very well in the landscape where temperatures stay above 10°F. If winters are too severe, a *Pachpodium lamerei* grows well in a container that can be moved to a more protected area or indoors with bright, indirect light. For planting techniques and care information, see pgs. 160-165.

LANDSCAPING TIPS & IDEAS

Aloe dichotoma (quiver tree) may be pricey because it is slow growing and relatively rare; however, for a stunning, unique landscape focal point in the southwestern United States or wherever temperatures remain above 27°F, it is worth the investment. *Euphorbia grandicommis* (cow horn plant) and *Euphorbia ammak* 'Variegata' (African candelabra or ghost euphorbia) make effective architectural and barrier plants because of their menacing spines and toxic sap.

ALL ABOUT

Bushmen use *Aloe dichotoma* (12–29 ft. x as wide) to make quivers for their arrows. Its distinctive appearance includes a stocky, pale trunk; flaking bark; rounded crown with a forked branching pattern covered by narrow, finger-like leaves; and yellow, tubular flowers with orange stamens in fall or winter. The North African

Common Name/Botanical Name
Quiver Tree
Aloe dichotoma

Euphorbia ammak 'Variegata' (up to 20 ft. x 8–10 ft.) has yellow to green branches growing near the top like a candelabra; in spring/summer small chartreuse-yellow flowers appear. *Pachypodium lamerei*, the Madagascar palm, is not a palm but a succulent with large 2 in. spines on a stout, gray trunk that can reach 10 ft. outdoors. Its foliage grows spirally at the top with fragrant flowers in summer. As a houseplant, it will grow 4–6 ft. and will not flower. From Kenya, *Euphorbia grandicomis* is an upright, multistemmed shrub with angular, zigzag-shaped stems and cowhorn-like spines. Tall, yellow flowers in late spring followed by purple fruits line up in rows on the angled ridges of the branches.

Agave Victoriae, page 22

Aloe ciliaris, page 23

Aeonium 'Kiwi', page 21

Epiphyllum, page 47

Senecio scaposus, page 26

Echeveria 'Perle von Nurnberg,' page 25

Crassula arboroscens, page 25

SUCCULENT "GROUT" FOR STEPPINGSTONES

Sedums, ice plants, sempervivums, and other succulent groundcovers used in this project provide visual interest to the landscape even when they're not in bloom. They require little maintenance while adding beauty to outdoor spaces. While the bulk of succulent groundcovers will not survive heavy foot traffic, they can be used as "grout" to fill in spaces between steppingstones or design geometric patterns in gardens.

Persevering attributes of heat- and drought-tolerance make succulents ideal choices as no-fuss fillers or groundcovers that carpet hillsides for erosion control. Many, such as Cooper's ice plant, *Delosperma cooperi*, and English stonecrop, *Sedum anglicum*, are hardy to Zone 5 and warmer.

PLANTS
Echeveria imbricata - Blue rose
Echeveria azulita

SUPPLIES
Garden steppingstones
Cactus mix soil

4 SIMPLE HOW-TO STEPS TO CREATE SUCCULENT "GROUT"

1 Prepare the ground by leveling the area and setting down the garden steppingstones.

2 Dig in between the stones, and plant succulents slightly lower than the steppingstones.

3 It is best to select low profile, slower-growing varieties of succulents.

4 Sprinkle pebbles in and around the succulents for a finished look, allowing the plants to spread over them.

HYPERTUFA PLANTER

How cool is it to create your own succulent containers! Hypertufa production is a lot of fun and a terrific way to bring the look of stone into the garden, without the weight (and not much "wait" either). Let your imagination run wild to choose intriguing, practical, one-of-a-kind shapes and images. Almost anything that has an interesting form, such as old Tupperware, beach pails, or used nursery pots, can be used as a mold.

Since this process can get messy, kids are more than willing to help. As long as they wear the protective gear, this project is a simple one to surreptitiously get them to spend a little time away from technology.

PLANTS
Graptosedum hybrid 'Alpenglow'
Senecio rowleyanus – 'String of Pearls'
Sedum spathulifolium 'Cape Blanco'
Echeveria imbricata – Blue rose
Crassula marginalis rubra variegata – Calico kitten
Echeveria 'Blue Curls'
Yucca gloriosa var. *recurvifolia* 'Bright Star'
Oscularia deltoides – Pink ice plant

SUPPLIES
Portland cement
Perlite
Peat moss
Water
Cooking spray
Assortment of large and small
  containers that nest within
  one another
Used or new wine corks
Heavy-duty gloves
Safety goggles
Safety mask
Measuring glass
Mixing tub
Rubber mallet
Bubble wrap or foam contact
paper for texture (optional)

A HYPERTUFA PLANTER

1 Measure out equal parts of Portland cement, perlite, peat moss, and water, and mix together in a large basin. Mix until all the ingredients are well blended into a "cottage cheese" consistency.

2 Spray the molding containers with cooking spray. To texturize the hypertufa exterior, add bubble wrap, spray heavily with cooking spray on the front and back, and place the bubble wrap around the container's outer edges.

1a

1b

2

3 Scoop the cement mixture into the larger container.

4 After a couple scoops of cement, add one or two wine corks all the way through the bottom for drainage. Make sure to spray the cork with cooking spray.

5 Continue filling the hypertufa mixture into the outer container until it is about ⅔ full.

6 Center and press the inner container into the outer container. If necessary, weight the nesting containers in place with a heavy rock. Press and fill hypertufa around all the edges up to the top; level and smooth off the rim.

DESIGNER NOTES
◆ **Protect yourself.** Make sure to wear a mask, protective eyewear, and long, heavy-duty, latex gloves.
◆ **Do not add too much water.** If the mixture seems too wet, add another cup of each ingredient until it feels right.
◆ **Remove the inner container after about 24 hours** to allow more air to complete the drying process from the inside out.
◆ **Cut the wine corks in half** before inserting into the bottom of the hypertufa (to make the drainage holes) if the design is shallower.
◆ **Allow 48 hours for the hypertufa to dry** completely; then, remove it from the inner and outer containers with a rubber mallet.
◆ **Allow about 3 weeks for the hypertufa to cure** before planting it.
◆ Turn the hypertufa container over and **pop out the cork(s)**.

GARDEN DOOR

Garden visitors are lured by the idea of exploration and a succulent "doorway" that welcomes them with a touch of whimsical intrigue and promises a memorable experience. The door makes a bold statement that screams "free-spirit" with an almost funky and energetic style. Your guests are sure to muse, "I want this door in my garden."

When decorating outdoor garden areas, many of the same design principles apply as they do inside the home. It helps to think of the garden as a room without a ceiling. When a garden displays a spontaneous mood and artistic fancy, folks are often drawn to the engaging results.

PLANTS

Euphorbia obesa – Basketball or baseball plant
Sedum spathulifolium 'Cape Blanco'
Echeveria imbricata – Blue rose
Aeonium 'Silver Edge'
Notocactus magnificus – Balloon cactus
Echeveria azulita
Agave victoriae-reginae – Queen Victoria agave
Aeonium arboreum var. *atropurpureum* 'Zwartkop' – Black rose
Aeonium percarneum 'Kiwi'

SUPPLIES

Solid wood door
Tools: jigsaw, sander, leveler, hammer, and shovel
Square floral containers or ¼-inch-thick, 1 x 2 in. wood and backing
Wood screws
Exterior paint
Primer
Paint brushes, roller, and tray
Exterior sealant
Door hardware
Exterior door hinges
4 x 4 x 8 in. post and finial
Cement
Cactus mix soil
Chicken wire
Staple gun

6 SIMPLE HOW-TO STEPS TO CREATE
A GARDEN DOOR

1 Start with a used or new unfinished wood door and sand down any residual paint or stain. Plan the configuration of planting space—how little or how much area for the plants compared to how much wood door will be exposed.

2 Using a jigsaw cut out panels or squares from your door and sand any rough-cut edges.

3 Clean, prime, and paint, or simply stain and seal. Be sure to use exterior paints and sealants for the garden door to weather the exposure to the elements and the watering of the plants.

4 On the back, build square planting beds measured to fit the planting openings or use a pre-manufactured shallow tray and attach to the back using wood screws as seen in the demonstrated project. A 12 x 12 in. shallow tray is commonly available at florist, craft, or building supply stores.

5 Drill drainage holes in the top, bottom, and sides of the planting trays. This will allow the succulents to take root and also allow for watering when they are in place. Watering is accessible from the top back side of the garden door. For a wooden tray, make sure to seal it with a spray sealant before planting as well as drilling drainage holes as described above.

6 Lay the door on a table and plant. Add chicken wire mesh securely on top of the planting tray above the soil to hold the plants or cuttings in place when standing the door. Attach the chicken wire with a heavy-gauge staple gun and staples.

3

DESIGNER NOTES

◆ Another option is to **hang the vertical door planter on a wall** by attaching heavy-duty picture mounting wire and screws and also using a strong toggle to secure the weight of the door.

◆ **Wood window frames and shutters** would also serve as a really interesting base for a vertical garden. Simply add a planting bed behind them.

◆ **To hang the door in place,** attach hinges just like a regular door and mount the opposite hinge to a 4 x 4 x 8 in. wood post. Mount the hinges while connected to ensure that they will line up correctly when installing the door in the garden. Allow for approx. 2 ft. of the post to be buried in the ground with concrete.

◆ Dig a hole for the post, balance the post in the hole, and fill with mixed concrete. **Use a leveler tool so that the post is set straight.**

◆ Once the post sets, **hang the door using the hinges and pins.**

4 **5**

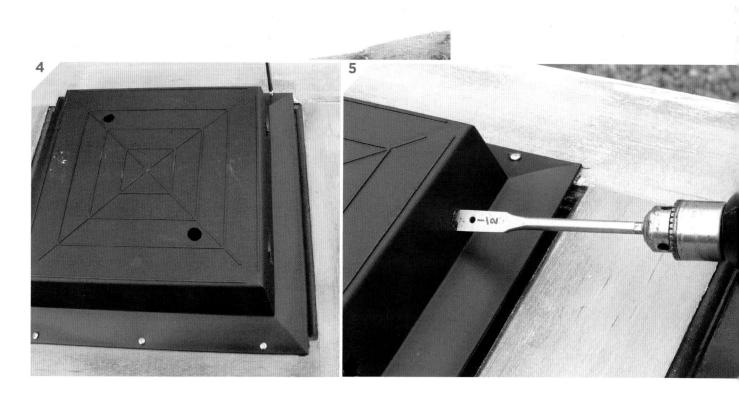

Whether on a sunny windowsill or in a greenhouse, on a patio or beneath a skylight, container-grown succulents offer all the pleasure of in-ground gardening at a more relaxed pace. These are plants that allow you to be lazy.

—Debra Lee Baldwin

PLANT ACCENTS THAT BLOOM THEIR HEADS OFF

A garden landscape with structural and textural succulent plants lends itself to simplicity and open space, an almost meditative Zen-like study of quiet contemplation where columnar, branched, and rounded silhouettes are the focus. But there is also the serendipitous arrival of reds, pinks, oranges, yellows, magentas, and greens, a riotous festival of floriferous color. Because of variations in soils and climates, not all plants featured here will grow and bloom in the outdoor garden. Some may bloom only if there is an extended period of heat, while others need cooler more moderate temperatures. Many flourish against the reflective heat of a wall or other structure; others prefer a bit of afternoon shade. And most need to be kept dry during their dormancy. Their specific cultural needs, however, can be accommodated if planted as container accents so they can be moved easily to a protected area during inclement weather or even indoors until outdoor conditions suit them better.

Think of a pot, basket, hypertufa trough, or a "repurposed" improvised picture frame, tree stump, or laundry tub as an empty canvas, just waiting for a palette of plants according to one's personal desire. Fortunately, because succulents are slow growing and do not require much root space, they can remain happily ensconced in a small pocket no more than 12 inches around and a depth of a few inches as long as they are in a fast-draining planting medium. And unlike other thirstier annuals and perennials, they do not require much tending or watering, in fact, they thrive on benign neglect.

Succulents grown primarily for their blooming accents rather than for their structure offer another avenue of creative experimentation. To help bring out the exuberant joyfulness of color, the following featured plant selections are not meant to be the end-all-to-be-all of container accents, but they are meant to inspire and nudge those who have not thought of succulents as blooming focal points. Unlike pedestrian marigolds or petunias found growing in grandma's garden, these are blooming accents that are extraordinarily fancy and fanciful.

Hybrids of *Adenium obesum* bear clusters of oleander-like flowers in brilliant hues of pink, red, or purple with darker throats or white and yellow throats, often edged in a deeper or contrasting tint as well as radiating stripes that rest atop a stout trunk like a glorious blossoming crown. Even their leaves can be green to variegated. Another take-your-breath-away plant is *Calandrinia spectabilis*, whether planted en masse in the landscape or potted up in containers to show off its satiny, cup-shaped magenta flowers standing tall and proud on wiry 18–36 in. stems that dance in the slightest breeze.

Then there are the easy-to-care for *Epiphyllum* hybrids that bear magnificent flowers, some measuring dish-sized 10 in. across, behemoths in every color of the rainbow except blue, as well as daintier 2–3 in.

blossoms. *Euphorbia milii* is a bit stingy with its foliage but more than compensates with clusters of bright red, yellow, orange, white, and pink bracts. For lovely thick, scalloped leaves and dainty clusters of flowers, *Kalanchoe blossfeldiana* is another specimen ideally suited for pot culture with yellow, red, pink, and orange double or single blossoms. Despite their spectacular blooms, they are all succulents with stems, branches, or both that store water during times of little or no rainfall. Blooming succulents help soften the often stark simplicity of their flower-impaired relatives and in containers, cultural requirements can be tailored to suit their unique demands.

Most important, containers spotlight their beauty for the eye of the beholder and can be as dramatic and beautiful as a pot full of traditional posies, minus the water and the work.

Botanical Name/Common Name
Adenium obesum hybrids
Desert Rose

Botanical Pronunciation
a-DEN-ee-um o-BEE-sum

the plants will shed their leaves, but where climates are mild and water is available, they will remain evergreen. Under ideal conditions similar to their native habitats, plants in the *Adenium* genus can reach 3–9 ft. tall and have distinctive pachycaul stems (thick-stemmed, often bottle-shaped trunks that are sparsely branched or unbranched), but in containers, they will remain evergreen.

ALL ABOUT

Recently, growers have developed many colorful, eye-candy hybrids that have been grafted onto a vigorous, seedling rootstock contributing to the popularity of *A. obesum* as a houseplant or bonsai in temperate climates. The bright red, pink, or purple blossoms are a stunning contrast to the smooth-barked, green to pale brown, bottle-shaped trunk. If grown indoors, plants need bright, indirect light, and temperatures no lower than 50°F. Also, rotate the container occasionally to discourage one-sided growth, and unless water is withheld, it will not go dormant in the fall. Plants can be grown outdoors in sun or partial sun, if there is no danger of frost, up against a heat-retaining wall, under a porch roof, or in filtered light near the edge of a protective canopy of a tree. When the temperature dips below 50°F, it is time to bring the plants indoors or into a well-insulated greenhouse. Wear heavy-duty gloves when handling *Adenium* species because of the toxic, milky white or translucent latex. In fact, in Africa, the sap from its roots and stems is used as an arrow poison for hunting large game and fish.

DESERT ROSE

Endemic to the deserts of Kenya, Tanzania, and Zimbabwe as well as the Arabian Peninsula, most *Adenium* species bloom in the late winter with pink or red, five-petaled tubular flowers that resemble oleander or plumeria blossoms. But unlike their cousins, *Adenium* species are succulent plants capable of storing water in stems and branches when there is scant or zero rainfall. Their leathery leaves grow in a spiral, gathering near or at the tips of the branches. During extended periods of drought or cold spells,

ROCK PURSLANE

For skeptics who assert succulents have few positive attributes except for their water-thriftiness, they have never seen this spectacular Chilean perennial in its full blooming glory. The common name is rock purslane, but there is nothing common about *Calandrinia spectabilis*. The satiny, 2-in. cup-shaped flowers may only remain open about one to two days, but there are up to 10 more buds waiting in line on 18–36-in.-long stems that open up one at a time providing a very long bloom period. Once mature, it will send up a plethora of flowering spikes over several months. No deadheading is necessary; just let it bloom away. Providing a lovely contrast to its flowers are low, dense rosettes of thick, grayish blue-green, narrow leaves with smooth margins. The spoon-shaped leaves are about 2 in. long and provide a soothing backdrop for the brilliant magenta flowers bouncing and waving on 1–2-ft. wiry stems. Once mature, the deer-resistant and easy care *Calandrinia* stands 10–12 in. tall with a 36-in. spread.

ALL ABOUT

From the hot, dry mountains of Chile, *C. spectabilis* is not only drought tolerant, but also requires almost no water once established. It is a no-brainer plant for the dry, Mediterranean garden and blends in perfectly with other succulents and cacti. As a dense groundcover, it stifles interloping weeds, and planted en masse in front of borders or in a rock garden, this magenta-flowering specimen is bound to win over any succulent skeptic from spring to fall. As an added bonus, butterflies and hummingbirds will flock to its floriferous display. In winter, to prevent leggy growth, cut it back by about 6 in. so it will look its best in spring. Cuttings can be transplanted in other sunny areas of the garden. It will not be hardy below 25°F, and where freezing temperatures are common, plant these bluish green rosettes in containers along with other low-water plants, coordinating with other blue-hued succulents or as a standalone specimen. Then move indoors or into a greenhouse during the frosty season.

Botanical Name/Common Name
Calandrinia spectabilis
Rock Purslane

Botanical Pronunciation
ka-lan-DREEN-ee-ah
speck-TAB-ih-liss

ORCHID CACTUS

A typical reaction when seeing an *Epiphyllum* hybrid for the first time is the question, "Orchid or cactus?" The common name for *Epiphyllum* is orchid cactus, and it is easy to think that the magically fluorescent flowers must be orchids rather than cactus. They are in fact tropical epiphytic cacti from South and Central America growing mainly in the crooks of trees forming flat, leaf-like, spineless green stems with scalloped edges growing about 2–6 ft. long. Not a climber, individual plants lean on a tree or other sturdy support. Like cactus, *Epiphyllum* species have modified leaves but, unlike desert cacti, have adapted to the humid, shady conditions of the tropics and are still protected from water loss. Although their stems are fascinating, they are grown for their spectacular and large 4–10 in. flowers blooming from spring to fall (although some hybrids bear smaller flowers). Attached to the end of a long tuber emerging from the side of a stem, a large cup miraculously opens up to reveal flaring silky petals centered with numerous filament-like stamens and a stigma. The species flowers open at night and close during the day, but most hybrids bloom during the day, come in every color of the rainbow except blue as well as bicolors, and some are even fragrant.

ALL ABOUT

Most of the brightly hued *Epiphyllum* species are hybrids as opposed to their paler cream or white-blooming nocturnal cousins. In Victorian times, hybrid crosses originated in Europe, but more recent breeding is being done in the United States, in particular California. Collectively, the hybrids are nicknamed "epis," and although considered a succulent, remember epis are tropical plants, not drought-tolerant cacti, and are more dependent on regular water. The long, arching stems with spectacular blossoms show off best in hanging baskets, large tubs, or pots. Indoors, combine them with other tropical plants or succulents, or place them outdoors on a partially shaded deck or under the protective canopy of trees. Where winters are cold, they can be overwintered indoors in bright, indirect light and taken outdoors after the danger of frost is past.

Botanical Name/Common Name
Epiphyllum hybrids
Orchid Cactus

Botanical Pronunciation
ep-ih-FILL-um

Botanical Name/Common Name
Euphorbia milii
Crown of Thorns

Botanical Pronunciation
you-FOR-bee-uh MILL-ee-eye

CROWN OF THORNS

Euphorbia milii is commonly known as crown of thorns because its stems and branches are armed with ½ in. thorns that ancient legend associates with the crown of thorns worn by Christ. In Thailand, the name for this species is "Poysean" because "poy" means "eight" and "sean" stands for "saint." It is their belief that if the plant bears eight flowers in a cluster, luck will follow. Native to Madagascar, this species is typically stingy with its foliage, but it more than compensates for its pairs of clustered, usually, red bracts that bloom on and off throughout the year at the ends of long peduncles (a stem that supports the bract or flower). What are mistakenly referred to as flowers are really colorful bracts surrounding the true flowers which are tiny and insignificant. Many varieties and hybrids are available from Asia, Europe, and the United States and come in a dazzling array of forms, sizes, and bract colors.

ALL ABOUT

Easy to grow and tolerant of seaside conditions, it does well in mild weather areas, but where cold winds or frosts are common; plant against a protective wall or in a container where it can be moved indoors and provide afternoon shade during hot, dry summers. The most common colored bracts are red and yellow, but exotic hybrids are now available with variegated leaves or larger and flashier bracts in fluorescent colors ranging from chartreuse to bold oranges, creamy white, and hot, hot pinks. The species has a sprawling growth habit from 1–4 ft. tall x 1½ ft. wide, but recent varieties are dwarf in habit, more compact, and more floriferous, making them ideal container plants. Although perfect in pots on the patio, it will thrive in rock gardens, along sunny borders, or in a seaside garden as long as there is no frost. And because of its armored thorns, *E. milii* is an effective hedge or barrier plant. As with most *Euphorbia* species, wear sturdy gloves to protect from thorns as well as its toxic, milky, latex sap that oozes from bruised or broken stems and leaves.

KALANCHOE

Another "ouchless" blooming accent, the Madagascar native *Kalanchoe blossfeldiana* bears lovely succulent foliage, often with glossy and smooth or scalloped edges or another unique form with umbels of petite flowers rising above the leaves. In its native habitat, it is found growing in semi-arid conditions where rainfall is less than 10–15 in. per year, an ideal plant for a Mediterranean climate or dry garden. With an upright, multibranched growth habit, it is very attractive, bearing primarily sparkling scarlet red, yellow, or orange flowers that last for weeks and bloom off and on from spring through the winter months. Flowers initiate after about 6 weeks of 14-hour nights in the winter and early spring. Although hardy from USDA Zones 10–12, it is happiest in warm, mild temperatures. At maturity, plants grow up to 18 in. tall and as wide, but some are sold as petite specimens in containers smaller than a teacup. The only caveat is to keep this species away from pets and small children because the plant and flowers contain cardiac glycosides which are toxic if ingested.

ALL ABOUT

With large clusters of flower heads, *K. blossfeldiana* is the most popular with consumers and comes in a variety of colors. Growers also appreciate the fact that they can "force" these plants to bloom just about any time of the year, although their natural flowering cycle begins in the late winter to early spring season. Recent hybrids have been introduced with different-sized and various-hued pink, salmon, creamy white, and bicolored flowers, singles and doubles, as well as leaves that may be a rich forest green or edged in festive red. For cooler climates, use them as indoor accent plants, but where evening temperatures are in the 60s and 70s during the day, they can remain outdoors. This species is ideal for sunrooms, bright windowsills, or on the porch or patio during mild weather, but if temperatures are too high or too low, plant damage and limited flower production may occur. Otherwise they are not fussy plants, needing only minimal care and fertilization, providing they are not overwatered, especially in winter.

Botanical Name/Common Name
Kalanchoe blossfeldiana
Kalanchoe

Botanical Pronunciation
kal-an-KOE-ee bloss-fel-dee-AY-nuh

In the midst of the word he was trying to say,
In the midst of his laughter and glee,
He had softly and suddenly vanished away—
For the Snark was a Boojum, you see.
                                    —Lewis Carroll, *The Hunting of the Snark*

WEIRDLY WONDERFUL COLLECTOR'S CHOICES

Succulents as a group are generally a collection of strange and wonderful things. Yet, even within this medley of curiosities, there exists a fascinating band of outlandishly delightful and captivating plants that are just weirdly wonderful. From the boojums of Baja to the bizarre *Welwitschias* of the Namib Desert, there are myriad succulent life forms that seem totally alien to the planet. They inspire in us a desire to collect and create.

Of course, the general belief that all succulents adapted to grow in desert environments is not correct. Many of them evolved in the cold, alpine regions of Europe, where they reconciled to the poor, rocky soil and strong winds. Other succulents restyled themselves in the rainforests of Central and South America and also adjusted to the beaches where the salt concentration was extremely high. Whatever environment succulent plants finds themselves in, their survival depends on a necessity to survive periods where water is not constantly available. This "drive to survive" in water-deprived areas brings an advantage of perpetuation of the species without an excess of competition to vie for limited resources.

The spread of succulents across the globe is as mystifying as the plants themselves. Cacti are New World plants and are native to only the American continents. While succulents are more widespread, with concentrations in southern and eastern Africa, virtually none are found on the continent of Australia. Major plant expeditions began in the late fifteenth century during the competition to find a western sea route to India. Christopher Columbus is credited with bringing the first cactus to Europe and presented these "shocking" leafless plants to Queen Isabella of Spain. Other explorers like Vasco de Gama discovered succulents in southwestern Africa and India.

Technology has made access to weirdly wonderful succulents easier than taking a dangerous botanical trek, and a few may even be found in one's local garden center. However, many types remain available to only the most dauntless of collectors and can become living trophies. Protection of these quirky succulents in their native habitats will help to ensure their survival, but it may fall to plant enthusiasts and their efforts at propagation to be the final safety net. Mimicry plants that resemble rocks are among those that may be most accessible to the average gardener. Their shape, size, and color cause them to resemble small stones in the landscape. Therefore, they are usually overlooked by moisture-seeking animals, which would otherwise eat them during periods of drought.

Euphorbia lactea 'Cristata Variegata', resembling marbled alabaster, is another living treasure that is easier to find but a little more costly than other succulents because of its slow growth rate. The intriguing climbing onion, *Bowiea volubilis*, may be procured with a little searching, but it is listed as Vulnerable in the 2009 IUCN Red List (the International Union for Conservation of Nature's Red List of Threatened Species) because of severe pressure from medicinal plant harvesting over most of its range in South Africa. *Haworthia truncata* is one of the more common oddities and may be found in most succulent enthusiasts' collections. It is an easily cultivated species, which can be propagated by seed, offsets, and leaf or root cuttings.

As accumulators of the twisted, many enthusiasts specialize in monstrose and cristate forms of succulents. With its yeti-like covering, *Espostoa ritteri cristata* does not fail to capture the imagination of the macabre. Also on the monstrose list is *Pachycereus schottii* monstrose, a rare, mutated form of the totem pole cactus that is thornless. Harder to procure for the collector are specimens of the stately boojum tree, *Fouquieria columnaris*, with its spectacular conical shape and branchlets spread somewhat regularly around the trunk. Another arboreal-type plant is the tree grape, *Cyphostemma juttae*, which can grow to 6 ft. and comes from the hot, dry areas in southern Africa. As with all hobbies there is a holy grail for succulent collectors: the unfathomable, *Welwitschia mirabilis*, which produces exactly two leaves in 1,000 years!

Common Name/Botanical Name
Alabaster Swirl, Elkhorn
Euphorbia lactea
'Cristata Variegata'

Botanical Pronunciation
yoo-FOR-bee-uh lak-TAY-uh

ALABASTER SWIRL

Euphorbia lactea forms beautiful alabaster marbled stems that branch to form candelabra specimens to 6 ft. in height. Alabaster Swirl is a crested form of *E. lactea* that has tortuous, undulating, fan-shaped branches of beautiful alabaster marbled with splashes of green that form a snaky ridge or congested growth clump. The causes of cristate versions of plants are generally unknown but may be due either to variances in light intensity or some type of physical damage to the cells at the tip of the branch. In reaction to the injury, growth begins to multiply at a much faster rate and the normal growing tip "goes crazy," creating fantastic whorls and fans. Unlike "monstrose" varieties of plants, where the variation from normal growth is due to genetic mutation, the crested forms may revert to normal growth for no apparent reason. If this occurs, it is necessary to remove the normal growth and leave the crested part behind. Recently, Thailand growers have produced new variegated cultivars ranging in color from white to yellow, pink, violet and green.

ALL ABOUT

Alabaster Swirl is easy to care for if a few basic guidelines are followed. While bright light is necessary, the plant will look its best if protected from strong sunshine in the hottest hours of the day. Water thoroughly when the soil is dry to the touch during the active growing period, which is in the late spring and summer months. In the winter months, watering should be severely restricted. Overwatering, especially during the winter months, is perhaps the most common failure in growing *E. lactea* 'Cristata Variegata', so supply the plant with porous soil with adequate drainage. Cold weather is another factor of which to be mindful. Since it is native to tropical Asia, this species is very tender and should be protected from frost. Typical of most euphorbias, the plant exudes a white milky sap when it's damaged. Many people are allergic to the sap and should rinse it off quickly if it comes in contact with the skin.

BOOJUM TREE

Baja California is so rife with peculiar plants that its landscapes often seem to be alien rather than earthly. Yet, even here, the boojum tree clearly stands out as the weirdest of the weirdly wonderful. *Fouquieria columnaris* is certainly one of the most outlandish appearing plants in the world. Shaped like spiny upside down parsnips, they never fail to grab the attention of the beholder. Some scientists speculate that this strategy maximizes exposure to the sunlight on all parts of the plant. Most plants grow in this erect and unbranched manner, but some bend over and even form loops, while others branch out into odd patterns. The boojum is fundamentally a type of ocotillo, *F. splendens*, differing from its kin in being a winter grower, whereas the ocotillo is spring and summer growing.

The common name comes from Lewis Carroll's *The Hunting of the Snark*. The book contains a mythical creature called the "boojum" that inhabited distant shores. When explorer Godfrey Sykes encountered the plants growing on the desolate Sonora coast in 1922, he was reminded of Carroll's story and christened these newly found succulents as boojums. It is now illegal to collect boojum tree seeds or plants from Mexico without permits from the Mexican government, so finding a nice specimen may require a little plant hunting by the collector.

ALL ABOUT

In the cool weather, when the plant is actively growing, water a boojum regularly, unless it is outdoors in a mild climate where winter rains may suffice. They need water every two to three weeks. However, small plants in pots may need water weekly. If leaves turn yellow or brown during this time, or begin to drop, it is usually a sign of too little water. In warm weather, boojum trees only need enough water to keep them from shriveling. Leaves, which turn yellow or brown and drop in late spring, are a sign that dormancy is beginning and excess water is detrimental at this point. Since plants are fairly slow growing, they will thrive in a container for a long time. Boojum trees are not particular about the type of soil as long as it has adequate drainage, so use a fast-draining soil or cactus mix when potting.

Common Name/Botanical Name
Boojum Tree
Fouquieria columnaris

Botanical Pronunciation
foo-KWEER-ree-uh kol-LUM-nair-iss

CLIMBING ONION

In a group of plants known for many interesting oddities, *Bowiea volubilis* is one of the great curiosities of the succulent world. It produces large onion-like bulbs that may measure from a few inches upward to as much as 10 in. across. Similar to onion and tulip bulbs, *Bowiea* bulbs are comprised of tightly clustered modified leaves, which serve as reserves of nutrients and moisture. Depending upon growing conditions, the bulbs may be consistently pale green or may be partially covered with the dried residue of the outer leaves. Over time, the bulbs eventually split to produce two bulbs and even more as the plant becomes very old.

The climbing onion has definite growth and dormant stages. During the active stage in late winter, *Bowiea* will produce long, entangled vines, which are actually the flower stems of the plant. As it matures, dense branches form and give the plant a full facade. Then, if the plant receives enough sunlight, myriad star-shaped, greenish-white flowers will scatter themselves along the stems. Unfortunately, their scent is as odd as the plant itself. When fall arrives, the growth dies back and the bulb goes into a resting period.

Despite its common name of climbing onion, all parts of a *Bowiea* are toxic and contain cardiac glycosides. They are only dangerous if eaten in large quantities but they may produce a minor skin irritation in people who have a sensitivity to the compounds. This species is listed as Vulnerable in the 2009 IUCN Red List (the International Union for Conservation of Nature Red List of Threatened Species) because of severe pressure from harvesting for medicinal plant use over most of its native range in South Africa.

ALL ABOUT

Remember that climbing onions thrive on neglect. They prefer well-drained, organic soil, and while they need regular watering during the growing season, allow the soil to dry before watering again. Once the

Common Name/Botanical Name
Climbing Onion
Bowiea volubilis

Botanical Pronunciation
BOW-we-a vol-OO-BIL-iss

stalk dries out after blooming, withhold all water until a new stalk begins to emerge in early spring. When regrowth does begin, provide the plant with a trellis or other vertical support so the vines can grow more upright. While the stems can grow quite long, they do not produce tendrils, so they can only stay in position by weaving their way through the stems of other plants or a support structure. This may be the number one choice for the beginning collector of weirdly wonderful plants because of its easy care, yet even experienced collectors will stop and admire a *Bowiea volubilis* in full growth.

Common Name/Botanical Name
Crested Peruvian Old Man
Espostoa ritteri 'Cristata'

Botanical Pronunciation
es-POS-toh-uh RIT-ter-ee

The swirling shapes of crested cacti are strangely beautiful, but add hair to them and they become as captivating as a Siren's song. It is not unusual for a succulent collector to become addicted to gathering only cristate and monstrose forms. The term cristation (or fasciation) describes a plant in which the growing tip is malformed due to the abnormal development of the apical meristem (a formative plant tissue usually made up of small cells capable of dividing indefinitely and giving rise to similar cells or to cells that differentiate to produce the definitive tissues and organs). When plant tissues begin to get overcrowded, they often seem to cease growth and several areas of normal plant material may shoot out from this crest formation. These areas should be quickly removed so the plant will continue to grow in the crested pattern.

ALL ABOUT

Like all cacti, *Espostoa* requires a sunny location and well-drained soil. But in summer, it appreciates fertilizer and wetter conditions. In winter, it needs a rest, but the temperature must not drop below 35°F. Initially it appears that many crested species grow faster, which is not surprising as there are many more growth points. It should not be unexpected that crested varieties of plants are a little more difficult to grow than their uncrested counterparts. Plant species have adapted themselves to growth rates that support their shapes and sizes. In nature, almost all mutations are detrimental to the survival of the species, and these crested cacti forms are no different. They are less adapted to their original environment but may be more easily perpetuated in a collector's care. Usually less water and plant food is needed for these mutant types. Since the plant's tissue is already growing in an unnatural manner, excess nutrients may cause the cactus to crack or rot as the process is accelerated. A general rule of thumb for care is, "If you are not sure whether to water or feed it, don't."

CRESTED PERUVIAN OLD MAN

Hairy cacti are incredibly captivating to gardeners of all ages. Like Cousin Itt from the fictional Addams Family, hirsute succulents are arguably the most enigmatic members of the cactus family. *Espostoa* is a genus of columnar cacti that is made up of 16 species endemic to the Andes of southern Ecuador and Peru. The genus is named after Nicolas Esposto, a noted botanist from Lima. *Espostoa ritteri* is an 8–12 ft. columnar cactus native to the Marañon Valley in Peru.

Common Name/Botanical Name
Horse Teeth Cactus
Haworthia truncata

Botanical Pronunciation
ha-WORTH-ee-a trunk-AH-tuh

HORSE TEETH CACTUS

Haworthia is a genus that comprises over 100 species of small succulent plants endemic to southern Africa. In appearance, many resemble miniature aloes, but others are comprised of leaves that look as if they have been roughly cut off at the tops and are positioned like a fan, not a rosette. Looking more like a piece of modern sculpture than a living plant, *H. truncata* is a marvelous example of the latter type. In habitat, it grows buried in the ground so that just the leaf tips are visible. Amazingly, the plant has the ability to pull itself even further into the ground during times of drought. The translucent, truncated leaf tips face upward and allow light into the interior chlorophyll-bearing layers of the plant where it may be captured for photosynthesis while avoiding water loss. This disappearing act also makes the plant less noticeable to moisture-seeking herbivores.

Under cultivation, *H. truncata* tends to grow above the soil. This better displays the unusual leaf form and arrangement, earning it the Afrikaans colloquial name *perderande*, or horse teeth. The Japanese breeders, who seem to have an innate ability to focus on particular groups of plants, have made *H. truncata* the subject of ardent breeding and selection, resulting in a number of wonderful cultivars with white lacy patterns on green-gray windowed tips, along with specimens of very unusual leaf shapes and sizes. While easier to obtain than other oddities, the horse teeth cactus remains curiously queer enough to be a superb addition to any collection.

ALL ABOUT

Perhaps the main care requirement for *H. truncata* is patience since it is not fast growing and requires several years to form impressive heads. Like other *Haworthia* species, it prefers locations of bright or filtered light rather than full sun. A fast-draining cactus mix should be used when potting. Plants should be watered more frequently in spring, and from late summer through fall, but a bit less in midsummer and kept fairly dry during the winter months in order to prevent rotting. Because haworthias are slow growing and for the most part stay small, a nice collection can fit comfortably on indoor windowsills. They can be easily grown as houseplants in colder climates and then vacationed as outdoor décor during the warmer months of the year.

Common Name/Botanical Name
Mimicry Plants (Living Stones)
*Lithops, Pleiospilos,
Fenestraria*, and others

Botanical Pronunciation
LY-thops, plee-oh-SPIL-os,
fen-es-TRAY-ree-uh

MIMICRY PLANTS

Living stones are some of the world's most fascinating plants! These queer little succulents have adapted themselves to resemble pebbles and rocks that litter their native habitats through southern Africa. For the most part, they are constructed of two fused succulent leaves that are connected to a long root. They have been referred to as "living stones" ever since their discovery by John Burchell in 1811, when "on picking up from the stony ground what was supposed a curiously shaped pebble, it proved to be a plant."

Mimicry of inanimate objects allows these succulents to blend into the landscape, and as with *Haworthia truncata*, this disappearing act makes the plant less noticeable to moisture-seeking herbivores. Each growing season, living stones develop a new set of leaves. The new leaves appear in the fall and are active through the winter and into summer. Dramatically, flowers appear near the end of summer or fall and are often larger than the plant itself.

ALL ABOUT

Succulent plant collectors avidly seek *Lithop* species and other mimicry plants. Their small size makes them ideal for collections that must be overwintered indoors in cold climates. They should be allowed to go drier in the winter when the new growth is drawing moisture from the old leaves. Water should only be sufficient to keep the root hairs alive, but do not allow the soil to become completely dry because the root hairs will desiccate and nothing will be present to absorb moisture. Most mimicry plants thrive in full sunlight, so provide as much light as possible. Weak light will cause etiolated growth (elongated leaves) and washed-out patterns on the leaves.

TOTEM POLE CACTUS

Continuing on with tales of the macabre comes the story of the fascinating totem pole cactus so called because of the multiple lumps protruding all over the cactus, giving the illusion of faces carved into the plant. It begins with Howard Gates, an American botanist and explorer as he travelled the Baja peninsula in 1931. While searching off primitive dirt roads, he came across a colony of bizarre and curious monstrose plants surviving in very soft sandy soil. This habitat is a fairly small area northeast of El Arco, which is about halfway down the Baja peninsula. The plants there are considerably weathered and marked with just the newest growing tips in acceptable condition. As this monstrose form of *Lophocereus schottii* does not flower, all specimens now in cultivation must have at one time been propagated vegetatively from plants in this area. The totem pole is so captivating that collectors owe a debt of appreciation to Mr. Gates for bringing this unique cactus into the marketplace.

Pachycereus (syn. *Lophocereus*) *schottii* is a model of a monstrose mutation in which the plants have lost their spines and all the edges are more rounded.

ALL ABOUT

In both the wild and with cultivated specimens, the stems mark quite badly due to blowing sand, weathering, and old age. It's hard to resist, but try not to handle them with bare hands. Any part of the cactus that gets oils from the skin may soon turn black and hard. Usually, only a few inches of growing stems remain in pristine condition. However, when grown properly, cacti make excellent landscaping and potted specimens. Follow the same care as with the recommendations for the crested Peruvian old man on page 56.

Common Name/Botanical Name
Totem Pole Cactus
Pachycereus schottii monstrose

Botanical Pronunciation
pak-ee-KER-ee-us SHOT-ee-eye

TREE GRAPE

Tree grape is an extraordinary succulent from South Africa and Namibia. It forms a bizarre canopy of serrated, blue-green leaves that emerge each spring from swollen, tree-like trunks. *Cyphostemma juttae* is a slow-growing succulent with a huge swollen trunk (a caudex, which makes this plant a caudiciform). These plants occur where they are exposed to very dry and hot conditions. Therefore, tree grapes have evolved and adapted amazingly well in order to survive. The presence of white, drooping, papery pieces of bark on the yellow-green stems is very typical of this species. In summer this shaggy-looking feature helps to reflect away the sunlight in order to keep the plant cool, and the thick, fleshy stems and leaves act as water reservoirs in times of drought. A fully grown plant can reach 6 ft. in height.

The toothed leaves are large and shiny during the spring and summer but fall off going into the winter months. The flowers are really not noticeable, but following them are large grape-like bunches of bright wine-colored berries that definitely attract attention.

ALL ABOUT

Cyphostemma comes from the hot, dry areas of southern Africa, so it has no problem taking temperatures up to 100°F; however, it may need some afternoon shade in hot climates to avoid leaf burn. It can handle winter temperatures a little below freezing, but it's best to protect it from frost, especially if the plants are young. As a slow grower, the tree grape can easily grow indoors in a pot. A fast-draining cactus mix should be used when potting. It is drought tolerant, but it appreciates some water and fertilizer during the summer growing season. Despite coming from areas that are dry in winter, it can adapt to wet-winter areas like coastal California. Plants should be watered more frequently in spring and from late summer through fall, a bit less in midsummer, and kept fairly dry during the winter months in order to prevent rotting.

Common Name/Botanical Name
Tree Grape
Cyphostemma juttae

Botanical Pronunciation
sy-foh-STEM-uh JOO-tay-ee

Common Name/Botanical Name
Tree Tumbo
Welwitschia mirabilis

Botanical Pronunciation
vel-VITCH-ee-uh mih-RAB-ih-liss

TREE TUMBO

Possibly the denouement of plant discoveries goes to one of the truly remarkable members of the plant kingdom. Often described as the "world's ugliest plant," *Welwitschia mirabilis* certainly ranks as one of the "most extraordinary plants on earth." Strange, unnatural, oddball, mysterious, fascinating, and grotesque are some of the words used to describe the tree tumbo. There really is nothing on earth like it. When first discovered by the Austrian botanist Friedrich Welwitsch in 1859, he stated that he "could do nothing but kneel down and gaze at it, half in fear lest a touch should prove it a figment of the imagination."

It is found and has adapted well to the harsh climate of the Namib Desert where virtually nothing else survives. Comprised of two leaves that capture moisture from sea fogs and long taproots (up to 90 ft. deep) that search out any underground water, *Welwitschia* is considered a dwarf tree or shrub that occasionally reaches a height of 6 ft. Some large specimens are believed to be 2,000 years old!

ALL ABOUT

While one might think *Welwitschia* plants should come with the warning "Don't grow this at home," that thought may not be accurate. If lucky enough to find it, *Welwitschia* can be grown somewhat easily, even as potted plants and even indoors in cooler climates. Once established, plants will grow steadily and are relatively disease free. However, since it is not a true succulent, it should not be treated as one. In the wild, it is dependent on water from its roots, and if grown in a pot, care should be taken that the soil does not dry out completely. There are three important factors to take into consideration if you're attempting to grow a *Welwitschia*. The first is the long taproot, so it needs a tall pot. Second, its reliance on extra moisture, so don't let the plant get too dry. Last is the soil, which should be typical of its native habitat. Plants from dry regions can be lost to funguses that live in highly organic soils. It is safer to use fast-draining, sandy mixtures and to water more frequently. Older plants tend to accumulate organic debris, which enriches the soil and acts as mulch, helping to retain water in the upper layers of the sand for a longer period of time.

Let no one think that real gardening is a bucolic and meditative occupation. It is an insatiable passion, like everything else to which a man gives his heart.

—Karel Čapek, *The Gardener's Year*

INTERIOR ACCENTS

During the '70s (actually a revival of a Victorian craze) houseplants were all the rage. Along with plant catalogs, they remedied the cabin fever of snowbound, frustrated green thumbs. As in the 1890s, Boston ferns, African violets, and philodendrons attempted to thrive in northern homes. However, indoor environments had changed dramatically. New heating systems created arid atmospheres lacking in the humidity necessary for healthy foliage to prosper. Exotic, fussy plants perished at rapid rates and disillusioned homeowners tired of the fad.

In the new millennium, as people grow weary of silk substitutes, there is a resurgence of interest in living plants to provide bright punches of color, to be given as gifts, and to maintain a serene and comfortable home. For all that, people want plants that fit into busier life styles and that will remain attractive without a lot of inconvenience. Enter succulents. Better fitted to modern lifestyles and living conditions, their popularity continues to increase.

This chapter demonstrates the easy steps required to create a dry terrarium or "xerisphere." For those that are a little quirkier, our project creator bejewels and bedazzles us with simple projects that look as if they came from a design magazine. All of this is done without the use of mundane tropicals, but with the incredible beauty of succulents that provide the "ooh and aah" of our xeriphytic designs.

While terrariums often conjure up images of miniaturized tropical scenes where water-loving plants are quite comfortable in highly humid environs, there are simple adaptations that can transform these enclosures to benefit desert dwellers. Perhaps the term for such a planter should more properly be coined as a "xerisphere" (from the Greek *xeros*, meaning "dry"). Unlike a terrarium, a xerisphere relies on the plants themselves to "camel" up and store the water.

Since succulents are naturally adapted to more arid habitats and are often slower growing, they are perfect choices for long-term living in glass enclosures. These xeriphytic plants require less water, less fertilizing, and less maintenance when displayed in such containers.

XERISPHERE DESIGNS BY PLANT TYPES

LARGE DOME
Dudleya hybrid
Euphorbia polygona
    'Snowflake' (cactus)
Tradescantia somaliensis –
    Kitten ears
Echeveria 'Black Prince'
    (*Shaviana* x *affinis*)
Sempervivum 'Pacific Devil's Food'

MINI DOME
Echeveria 'Azulita'
Haworthia fasciata – Zebra plant

LARGE 12-INCH BUBBLE BOWL
Echeveria harmsii – Plush plant
Portulacaria afra – Elephant bush
Sedum rubrotinctum – Pork-n-beans
Opuntia vestita cristata – Clothed opuntia (cactus)
Sempervivum calcareum – Hens and chicks

MEDIUM 8-INCH BUBBLE BOWL
Kalanchoe tomentosa – Panda plant
Mammillaria matudae cristata – cactus
Echeveria 'Black Prince'

MEDIUM 8-INCH BUBBLE BOWL – DEMONSTRATED PROJECT
Echeveria shaviana 'Truffles'
Crassula marginalis rubra variegata – Calico kitten
Senecio haworthia – Cocoon plant
Aloe brevifolia – Crocodile plant

SUPPLIES
Glass bowls (various sizes)
Dark-colored rocks
Horticultural charcoal
Cactus potting mix
Soil topper of choice (rocks, floral moss, tree bark,
    glass beads, or decorative sand)

EASY-CARE AND UNIQUE XERISPHERES

1a Choose a clear container (stay away from colored or smoky glass), and start by adding a ½-in. layer of small gravel or rock at the bottom of the container. This allows some water to move away from the soil in case too much is added.

1b Choose a dark-colored rock so that it virtually disappears in the soil line. If adding natural or colored horticultural sand (never beach sand, because of the salt) around the edges, make sure to complement your colored rocks or gravel with the sand.

1c Mix a layer of horticultural charcoal with or add it on top of the rock. Horticultural charcoal filters the water and keeps the xerisphere fresh and healthy. Horticultural charcoal can easily be bought online, or purchase "activated carbon" at a local pet store.

1

2 Add a thin layer of well-draining soil, such as a commercial cactus mix, for the roots to grow into. If adding sand to the project, keep the soil in the middle and gently pour a buffer or curb of sand around the edges. More sand can be added after succulents are planted to complete the look.

3

3a Now comes the fun! Select favorite succulents including cacti to make a creative desertscape. Wear protective gloves if handling spiny, "untouchable" cactus! While they may have hurtful spines, many have interesting shapes, textures, and flowers that are worth the extra protective effort.

3b Choose succulents that are hardy. Some of the more delicate succulents tend to get soft and struggle in a bowl-style garden, but *Haworthia*, *Aloe*, and *Sempervivum* species do very well.

4

5

4 Have fun with the planting, but remember all things beautiful in nature grow from the inside out, so work from the center and build out. Before adding a plant, break away the pot soil from around the roots so the succulent sits well in the arrangement. Add soil as needed to allow the plant to survive and help position the plants.

5 For the final step, select a soil topper of choice and fill in any exposed areas inside the garden. Rocks look very clean and natural, but floral moss, tree bark, glass beads, or decorative sand are allowed to suit the wildest of imaginations.

DESIGNER NOTES

◆ **Do not overwater.** Many containers do not have drainage holes, plus they are planted with water-thrifty succulents. So water once a month with a splash of purified or distilled water (to prevent salt buildup) around the base of each succulent; moisten just enough so that the plants are not standing in water.

◆ **Place in a sunny room with indirect bright light.** Succulents love light and need 4–6 hours of bright, indirect light every day to thrive, but direct sunlight may burn the plant.

◆ **Xerispheres often have a variety of unique succulents.** Depending on the variety, some are faster growing than others; the faster-growing plants may need an occasional trim with scissors or long-neck tweezers.

◆ **Lift the glass container from the bottom.** Never lift glass containers by the lip because they are often hand blown and the heavy weight of rocks, soil, and plants makes lifting from anywhere other than the bottom dangerous.

GLAMOROUS BEJEWELED GARDEN

It is probably a commentary on modern civilization that designer pet apparel is now a sizable business. While there is really no pressing need to improve on the natural order of things, humanizing animals helps many people identify with their pets. It might even be argued that a dog is just a plant without cell walls. Why not carry this theory of fashion and relativity into the succulent realm?

Our jeweled projects may not be for everyone, but they are simple, elegant, and downright astonishing! Like living works of art, succulents with a little bling are sure to get attention and appreciation, if not total understanding.

PLANTS
Crassula falcata – Propeller plant
Echeveria agavoides 'Red Tip'
Crassula – Jade plant
Sedum hybrids

SUPPLIES
Green floral wire, or thin gauge wire
Wire cutters
White glue
Adhesive-backed crystal ribbons
Glass marbles

GLAMOROUS BEJEWELED GARDENS

1a To attach beads on the tips of the succulent leaves, insert a thin gauge floral wire into the succulent's tip.

1b Snip the end off, leaving enough wire protruding from the tip to attach the bead.

2 Add a drop of simple white glue.

3 Slide the bead onto the wire and into the glue; allow it to dry.

4 Once all the beads are attached securely, plant the succulents in the garden.

5 Add glass marbles to cover the soil surface for a "glam" bejeweled garden.

DESIGNER NOTES

◆ **Use preglued beaded trims and appliques.** Another option is to use beaded trims and appliqués that are preglued, easy to peel off, and can be stuck directly onto succulents (available at a craft or hobby store in the scrapbook section).

◆ **Make sure to use a thin-gauge wire.** When inserting wire into succulents, use a thin gauge because if the wire is too thick, it will scar that area.

Now have fun and explore all the sparkling, bejeweled choices!

CLAY DISH GARDEN WITH SIDE HOBNAIL CONTAINERS

This design idea uses a mottled clay container, but the supplies and how-to directions are the same as for the Glamorous Bejeweled Garden (see pgs. 72-73).

PLANTS

Echeveria purpusorum
Kalanchoe panamensis
Sedum hybrid 'Burrito'
Euphorbia flanaganii cristata 'Green Coral'

DESIGNER NOTES

◆ **Do not overwater!** Typically a dish garden will need a little water every other week. With your finger, check the soil for moisture first to make sure it has dried out before being tempted to water again.

◆ **Keep the dish garden in a bright room.** Cacti and succulents require at least four hours a day of bright, indirect light.

WEDDINGS, PARTIES, AND SPECIAL EVENTS

Whether planning for a wedding, party, or other special event, there are so many decisions to make: theme, menu, beverages or cocktails, invitations, color scheme, traditional or cutting-edge or something in between, and, of course, cost.

A mind-boggling array of amazing, tempting, and over-the-top party options abounds, from caviar tastings to three-color origami letterpress invitations, in-house bartenders, musicians, and professional party planners. . . . And they all come with jaw-droppingly expensive price tags. If the budget is about to burst and the heart is suffering from sticker shock, the question that needs to be asked is will those must-haves truly add to the memory-making party. If the answer is, "Not really," then do a reality check by simplifying the celebratory event, including designing and making the floral displays.

The following projects illustrate the versatility of succulents as key components in floral arrangements that along with the company of good friends and family will be the toast of the special event. Mixed with cut flowers, they can add a new dimension, shape, and texture to the creative process and then can be separated after the celebration, rerooted, and planted for a perennial "happily ever after" life in the garden or in containers. Satisfying, budget-stretching DIY, stunning beauty, and repurposed plants—all are important reasons to say, "Let's party!"

HERE COMES THE BRIDE (AND BRIDESMAIDS TOO!)

BRIDAL BOUQUET

Succulent bouquets are among the hottest trend in wedding planning. The plants come in a countless mix of sizes and shapes, are fascinating to look at, and add a modern accent to any wedding décor. They can stand alone, but they also work beautifully in combination with fresh blooms like roses or mums.

Because they are available year-round, they are can be used in a celebration for any season and they will look just as good at the end of the night as they did during the day. Succulents provide a nice memento for guests, too, and are a great way to make a wedding eco-friendly since they can be replanted and become part of a couple's first garden. What a great gift!

PLANTS
Mini calla lilies
Freesias
'Sexy Pink', or other pink roses
Oceana roses (apricot-colored)
Craspedia—Billy balls (yellow ball-like flowers)
Snapdragons
Tulips

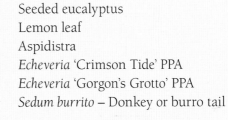

Seeded eucalyptus
Lemon leaf
Aspidistra
Echeveria 'Crimson Tide' PPA
Echeveria 'Gorgon's Grotto' PPA
Sedum burrito – Donkey or burro tail

SUPPLIES
Heavy-gauge floral wire
Sturdy wire cutters
Green floral tape
Florist picks (wired, green, wooden picks 4–8 in.)
Green chenille pipe cleaners
Orchid support stems
    (16- to 18-in., extra-long florist picks)
Ribbon

10 SIMPLE HOW-TO STEPS TO CREATE
A BEAUTIFUL BRIDAL BOUQUET

1 Remove the grower pot along with all the soil from your succulent.

2 Thread a heavy-gauge, 12-in.-long floral wire through the top of the succulent stem about half way.

3 Fold the wire, creating a "stem" about 6 in. long.

4 Add a floral pick or stake for additional stability and length needed when making the bouquet.

5 Secure the wire and pick together using floral tape. Floral tape sticks to itself and stretches as you wrap.

6 Continue to wire and tape each succulent necessary to make your bouquet.

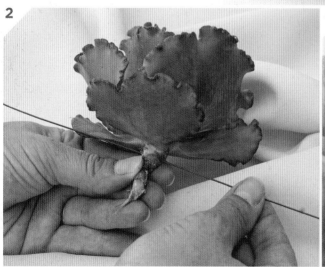

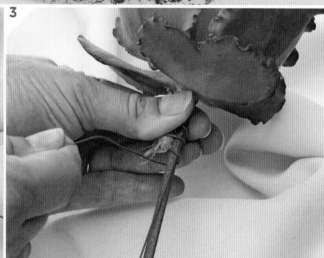

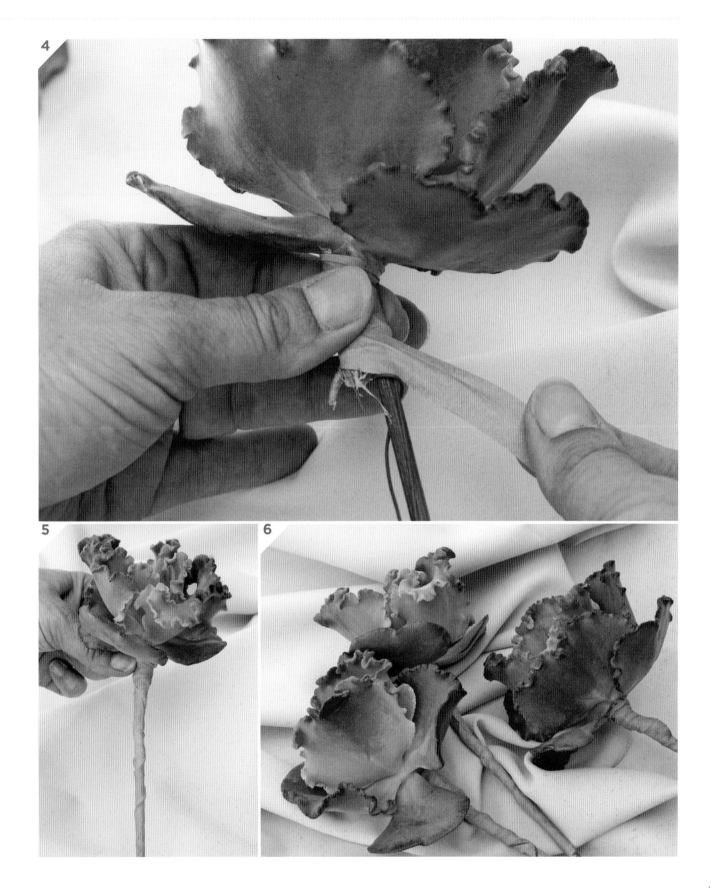

7

8

9

7 Once your succulents have "stems," arrange them just like adding a long-stemmed flower.

8 Add flowers using the same wiring and taping technique to fill in a nosegay-type, rounded shape; remember to keep holding the arranged stems in one hand while adding more stems with the other.

9 Tie the bouquet together using green chenille pipe cleaners.

10 Trim the stems even, wrap the top portion of the stems with ribbon, and place the bouquet in a water-filled vase until ready to use (don't let the ribbons sit in the water).

10

DESIGNER NOTES

◆ **Wire the succulents well in advance** of the big day. Store them by a bright sunny window to make sure they do not stretch or lose color.

◆ **After the event, pull off all the wire and tape.** Allow the succulent to callus over for about a week or two where there is bright, indirect light until the little pink baby roots emerge. Place it on top of cactus and succulent soil, and it will resurrect itself as a plant again.

◆ **Select succulents that can be handled** rather than the very fine powdery finish varieties that show fingerprints. *Sempervivum* species and *Haworthia* are hardy and look really great in boutonnieres and corsages.

◆ Once the succulents are added to the bouquet, it is okay to **place the bouquet in the refrigerator** to keep the flowers fresh. The succulents can survive the cold temporarily (up to 24 hours).

◆ Although this design was for a bridal bouquet, **the size or floral varieties and colors can be modified** for the bridesmaids or for a different festive occasion. The how-to remains the same.

FASCINATING FASCINATORS

Originally, fascinators were millinery pieces of fine lace, comparable to shawls, which always had lots of feathers. As a result of the public's infatuation with the British royal wedding and Kate Middleton's penchant for elaborate hair ornamentation, a modern fashion trend of hair accessories with elaborate trimmings is the rage once again.

Now a fascinator is often worn instead of a hat on occasions such as weddings, where hats were traditionally worn, or as an evening accessory. While these exotic decorations are meant to make a statement, how much more "fascinating" they become when living succulents are incorporated into the design!

PLANTS
Echeveria 'Perle Von Nurnberg'
Senecio haworthii – Cocoon plant

SUPPLIES
Hair combs
Narrow satin ribbon
Needle & thread
Low-temperature glue gun
Low-temperature glue sticks
Feathers
Jewels
Ribbon
Stemmed pearls
Sinamay (natural fiber ribbon)
Fascinator base
Floral tape
Floral wire
Wire cutter
Scissors

FASCINATING FASCINATORS

1 Prepare the base by attaching the fascinator to a hair clip/barrette, headband, or Sinamay millinery base, or simply use bobby pins to secure it into hair. Using a comb, start by weaving the fabric ribbon all around the top edge of the comb, sliding the ribbon between the comb teeth so that the floral and succulent creation can be sewn and attached securely on the ¼-in. plastic comb top.

2 Cut two rectangular pieces of felt fabric approximately the same size as the comb, and glue one of them to the top of the ribbon-wrapped comb. Save the other piece for later. With a needle and thread, stitch the felt fabric to the ribbon-wrapped comb.

3 To prepare the succulents, remove all of the soil from the plants and clean off the lower growth. Trim the roots, leaving a small stem. Using floral wire, pierce the top of the succulent stem, and push a 6-in. piece of wire halfway through. Bend the wire vertically down both sides creating a "stem." Wrap tightly from top to bottom with floral tape (floral tape feels like paper tape, but when gently pulled, it stretches and sticks to the wired stems as they are wrapped). Repeat wire and tape stem-making process for all succulents and succulent leaflets, as well as ribbons, beads, and any additional decorative accoutrements.

1

2

3a

3b

3c

4 Wrap the wired stems together with the floral tape as the fascinator is being created.

5 Cut the ends short with heavy-duty wire cutters.

6 Glue the other piece of cut felt to the back of the mini bouquet with one line of low-temperature hot glue. (Adding too much glue will make it difficult to sew to the other fabric.)

7 Glue and stitch together the comb and mini bouquet until tight and secure. To camouflage any exposed floral tape, add more ribbons or feathers.

4

5

6

7

DESIGNER NOTES

◆ **Use succulents that are resistant to fingerprints and that are more pliable** such as the varieties listed under Try These Yourself. This project requires a lot of handling, and succulents with brittle foliage tend to break too easily.

◆ Attach jewels, ribbons, and feathers into the mini bouquet by **using a low-temperature hot glue.** Avoid burning the succulents with the glue gun. The slightly lower temperature is less likely to scorch the succulents.

◆ The fascinator can be made days or even weeks before the main event as long as it is **stored where there is bright, indirect light.**

◆ **French wired-edge ribbons work best** for curling and keeping their shape. Sometimes the process of inserting them into the hair smashes the bows and tufts; they can be reshaped to their original beauty because of that wire.

◆ For other festive occasions, simply **change out the ribbons, pearls, and so forth** to create a less "bridal" design.

FASCINATORS, VEILS, HATS & HEADBANDS

PLANTS
BLACK & RED HEADBAND
Haworthia fasciata – Zebra plant
Echeveria multicaulis

**BROWN & GREEN HEADBAND
WITH BLACK FEATHERS**
Echeveria affinis 'Black Knight'
Haworthia reinwardtii hybrid

BIRDCAGE BRIDAL VEIL
Sempervivum arachnoideum 'Cobweb'
Sempervivum 'Green Wheel'

JUTE HEADBAND
Kalanchoe tomentosa
'Chocolate Soldier'

TAKING CENTER STAGE: THE CENTERPIECE

While eco-friendly weddings are decidedly "in," that in no way excuses a lack of the dramatic in centerpieces for the event. Our suggestions for combining succulents with traditional flowers allow breathtaking combinations that will not add extra expense to one's budget, but are sure to delight the eye of every guest.

This centerpiece project was specifically designed for a wedding; however, the size, elements, and flower varieties can be adapted to almost any occasion. And regardless of the celebration, as noted in our other wedding projects, the succulents can be re-rooted and grown to provide a keepsake of the occasion.

PLANTS
Hydrangea
Dianthus barbatus 'Green Trick'
'Ocean Song', or other lavender-colored roses
'Cool Water', or other bluish lavender-colored roses
Hypericum – Coffee bean berries
Wax flower
Lemon leaf
Lisianthus (purple)
Bells of Ireland
Stock (lavender)
Echeveria 'Perle Von Nurnberg'
Echeveria 'Tsunami'
Echeveria 'Aquarius'
Echeveria 'Lola'
Echeveria 'Lime & Chili'
Echeveria shaviana 'Truffles' (6 in.)
Echeveria imbricata – Blue rose
Echeveria 'Cameo'
Sedum mats

SUPPLIES
Low floral container (about 11–12 in. diameter)
Oasis floral foam (2 bricks/blocks)
Floral tape
Heavy-gauge wire
6-in. glass bubble bowls
Spanish moss
Sand-blasted grapewood (available at craft or florist supply store)

TAKING CENTER STAGE: THE CENTERPIECE

1 Remove the grower pot along with all the soil from the succulent.

2 Thread a heavy-gauge, 12-in.-long floral wire through the top of the stem, about halfway.

3 Fold the wire, creating a "stem" about 6 in. long.

4 Add a floral pick or stake. This will allow you to insert the succulent as you would a flower stem.

5 Secure the wire and pick together using floral tape. Floral tape sticks to itself and stretches when wrapped.

6 Continue to wire and tape each succulent for the arrangement.

7 When all the succulents have "stems," they can be arranged just like traditional cut flowers.

8 For weddings or any special occasion, this arrangement and its designer will receive tons of compliments!

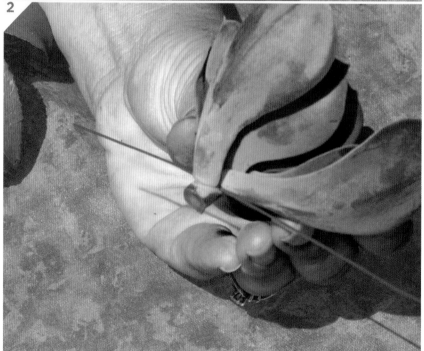

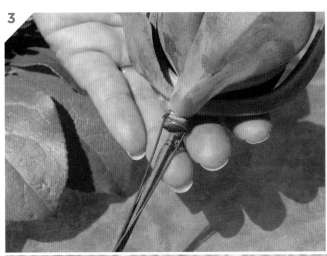

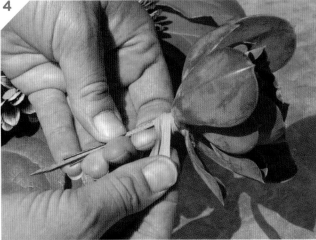

DESIGNER NOTES

◆ As with the bouquets, **wire the succulents ahead of the event** to save time for other preparations. Store where there is bright, indirect light to keep the plants from getting leggy or losing their color.

◆ **After the event, pull off all the wire and tape;** allow the succulent's cut end to callus over for about a week or two where there is bright, indirect light until the fine roots emerge. Place it on top of cactus potting soil, and it will root to become a plant once again.

◆ **Be sure to select plants that are sturdy enough for handling,** and try to stay away from varieties with a powdery finish that show smudged fingerprints.

BUOYANT ENCHANTMENT

Sometimes a special occasion allows—if not outright demands—a brazen display that laughs at the confines of tradition. This floating arrangement not only allows the hosts to strut their succulent "swagger," but it also evokes a childlike sense of wonder in the process. Guests may ask, "What is keeping that arrangement from sinking, and why is it in the pool?"

An evening affair can be made even more dramatic by adding candlelight to the arrangement, without falling into the routine practice of placing floating candles in the pool. This project definitely allows your creativity to come into play. Use an eclectic mix of components or go monochromatic with different shapes and sizes.

PLANTS

'Ocean Song', or other lavender-colored roses
Gaultheria shallon – Lemonleaf
Chrysanthemum
Echeveria 'Aquarius'
Echeveria 'Lola'
Echeveria 'Perle Von Nurnberg'

SUPPLIES

2-in.-thick, 8- to 24-in.-diameter
    Styrofoam wreath form
Wood picks
Fern pins

4 SIMPLE HOW-TO STEPS TO CREATE
FLOATING ARRANGEMENTS

1 Remove the lemon leaves from their stems, and pin them into the edge of the Styrofoam form with fern pins, overlapping slightly to cover the edge of the Styrofoam.

2 Prepare the succulents and flowers by inserting a wood pick into the bottom. Gently hold the succulent or fresh-cut flower by the head, and firmly press in the wood pick.

3 Then poke the flower heads and succulents into the wreath form, making sure to completely cover the base.

4 Optional: Add decorative trims and ribbons as desired.

DESIGNER NOTES
◆ **Perfect for a pool, pond, or fountain.**
◆ **Do not add too much weight to any one side.** Styrofoam floats easily above the water level. If the surface weight is evenly dispersed, the floating arrangement will balance perfectly.
◆ Arrangements of this nature are meant **for special events or one-day use only.** The roses and flowers are out of water and will last just a couple of days.
◆ The **succulents can be prepped in advance**, but leave the fresh flowers for last.
◆ To **center the arrangement** in a body of water, attach a clear plastic bag filled with white rocks. The white rocks will disappear against the white or light-blue bottom of a pool.

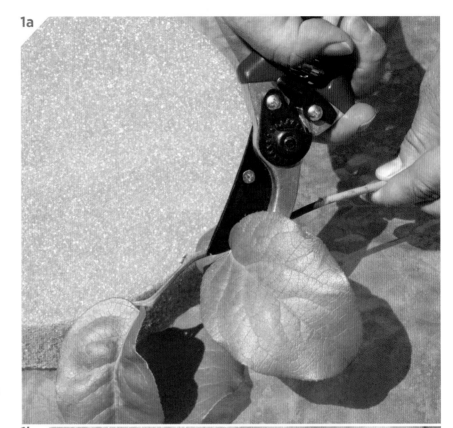

1a

1b

LIFE IS A BALL!

Hanging glass terrarium balls are a popular contemporary accent, but our twine project gives a natural, earthy feel to the concept. As we know, the first rule with growing succulents is that they need quick drainage. Twine balls are the *perfect* solution to maintain this requirement as the plants are less likely to be overwatered while suspended in space. Air plants and other epiphytes can also be added to create miniature landscaped worlds.

Twine balls are versatile and can be easily decorated for holidays or seasonal display. They can simply be brought indoors to overwinter in colder climates, but remember to hang them in a brightly lit area and reduce the watering.

PLANTS
Sedum
Echeveria 'Perle Von Nurnberg'
Echeveria shaviana 'Truffles'
Echeveria 'Dondo'
Haworthia 'Devil's Food'
Sempervivum arachnoideum 'Cobweb'

SUPPLIES
Barked wire twine
    (grass-wrapped heavy-gauge wire made by Oasis Floral Supplier)
Small 4-in. inflated toy ball
X-Acto or utility knife

LIFE IS A BALL!

1 Wrap the toy ball with the barked wire twine, and secure it with a triple twist at the top.

2 Continue to wrap the twine around the ball about 10–15 times until it resembles a wrapped ball of yarn. Be careful not to overwrap to allow room to reach inside the ball.

3 When finished, snip the wire and set the roll of twine aside. Make a small loop from the excess twine on the ball for hanging it later.

4 Cut an X in the ball with an X-Acto knife to deflate it.

5 Extract the deflated ball through one of the spaces between the twine rings. Use caution not to collapse the "walls" of the ball shape during this step.

6 Lay some moss or coco mat at the orb's base to hold the soil and cuttings in place.

7 Add a small assortment of succulents and cover the soil with remaining moss.

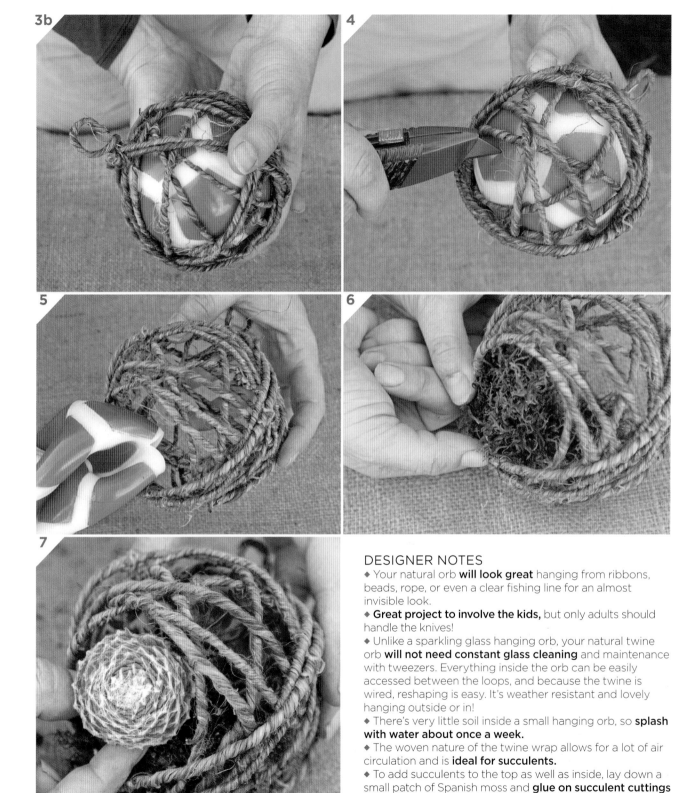

DESIGNER NOTES

◆ Your natural orb **will look great** hanging from ribbons, beads, rope, or even a clear fishing line for an almost invisible look.

◆ **Great project to involve the kids,** but only adults should handle the knives!

◆ Unlike a sparkling glass hanging orb, your natural twine orb **will not need constant glass cleaning** and maintenance with tweezers. Everything inside the orb can be easily accessed between the loops, and because the twine is wired, reshaping is easy. It's weather resistant and lovely hanging outside or in!

◆ There's very little soil inside a small hanging orb, so **splash with water about once a week.**

◆ The woven nature of the twine wrap allows for a lot of air circulation and is **ideal for succulents.**

◆ To add succulents to the top as well as inside, lay down a small patch of Spanish moss and **glue on succulent cuttings with white glue.** The roots will grow right into the moss.

RAISE THE WROOF!

Green rooftops are fast becoming the poster children for the ecology movement. Basically, a green roof is another way to garden vertically by installing a carpet of edible or ornamental plants (or both) on top of a roof. There are countless books and magazine features replete with photo layouts and directions touting the advantages of rooftop gardens, from providing access to outdoor green space for the home or work environment, improving air quality, and reducing carbon dioxide emissions to controlling storm water runoff and insulating buildings. For most of us, the problem is not only of cost, but also the headaches of engineering plans and adherence to local ordinances as well as installation and maintenance considerations.

If the planning, execution, and cost seem too daunting a springboard into the pool of eco-conscientiousness, there is a way to dip one's "toes" into rooftop gardening without diving in completely. Why not try a smaller scale project for Bowser? And if that seems too grand a scale, downsize even more by creating a roof for Tweety Bird or for the "you've got mail" box.

A DOGHOUSE OR BIRDHOUSE SUCCULENT ROOFTOP

PLANTS
Echeveria nodulosa
Cotyledon ladismithiensis – Fuzzy bear paws
Echeveria x 'set-oliver'
Sedum x *cremnosedum* 'Little Gem'
Echeveria affinis 'Black Knight'
x *Sedeveria* 'Jet Beads'
Echeveria setosa ciliata – Woolly rose
Sedum rubrotinctum – Pork-n-beans
Sedum mats

SUPPLIES
1x3 wood boards
Spray can of rubberized waterproof sealant
1¼-in. wood screws
Drill or screwdriver
Table saw or miter box and handheld saw
Exterior paint
Bowser's existing doghouse or a new one, or a birdhouse

A DOGHOUSE OR BIRDHOUSE SUCCULENT ROOFTOP

1 Measure the rooftop length, width, depth, and angle. Cut the boards accordingly to build and add a planting tray around the top of the structure. Align your corners and construct your joints based on preference and skill.

2 Drill holes in the bottom board to allow for proper water drainage.

3 Seal off the rooftop with spray waterproof sealant or staple a plastic liner instead, but make sure the drainage holes are free and clear.

4 Add a strip of common window screen across the drilled drainage holes to prevent soil from draining out when watering plants.

5 Paint the new trim to match or accent the doghouse. Make sure to use an exterior paint that will hold up outside. Depending on the color, it may need two coats.

1a

1b

6 Fill the tray with soil and plant. When planting at a steep slant, start at the bottom and work all the way up and across, filling with extra soil as each area is completed.

Optional: To give the roof a finished look, add a soil topper to cover any areas with exposed soil.

Note: If this is the first time experimenting with rooftop planting, try a smaller scale project such as a birdhouse or mailbox. Just follow the same step-by-step as the doghouse, only in miniature size.

DESIGNER NOTES

♦ To keep the rooftop "paw-fect" or "tweetable," the depth of the wood used to build the planting tray can be increased: **the deeper the tray, the more soil it will accommodate** and the less replanting it will need throughout the year.

♦ The caveat is that it will increase the weight of the topper, so **make sure the selected roof is sturdy enough** to support the weight before putting the project together.

♦ Similar to large home and commercial building rooftops, the plantings on top of Bowser's abode help to insulate his home, keeping him **cooler in summer and warmer in winter.**

6a

6b

A life-long blessing for children is to fill them with warm memories of times together. Happy memories become treasures in the heart to pull out on the tough days of adulthood.

—Charlotte Davis Kasl

KID-FRIENDLY PROJECTS

Today's child has a wonderland of toys to play with as well as video games, electronic tablet apps, and television programs. While all these gadgets, games, and shows are entertaining (think Angry Birds and all the variations), it is important to become "unplugged" and to be able to spend meaningful time together without the interface of a screen or earbuds. To encourage a life into the real, active world, tempt children with making things. Besides activating the youngster's creative juices, it is also an opportunity to spend time doing something together, a priceless chance to make memories.

Craft projects are the perfect activities to transform an average day into a fun day for the adult and for the child. If allowed to create and enjoy, youngsters will find there is a whole world out there that does not rely on electronic gizmos to have fun. Succulent plants combine perfectly with kid-friendly projects such as the African safari garden and the chalkboard living artwork to brighten any room. In the process, the kids will learn about the succulent plant kingdom, watch them grow, and learn how to care for them. *Furaha ya upandaji!* (That means "happy planting" in Swahili!)

AFRICAN SAFARI GARDEN

Involving children in fun gardening activities provides priceless opportunities to compete with technology and instill a love of nature into the younger generation. The joy of creating a living world from succulent plants is an activity they are unlikely to forget.

Children of all ages will have fun re-creating a miniature African savannah with a suitable succulent landscape. Fairy gardens have dominated the container scene in recent years, but constructing them is a bit like playing with dolls. Working with the wild animals of the Dark Continent may be a little more macho, but the educational opportunities for boys and girls are equally attractive.

PLANTS
Euphorbia spiralis
Rhipsalis mesembryanthemoides –
　　Clumpy mistletoe cactus
Sedum hernandezii
Sedum x *Cremnosedum* 'Little Gem'
Haworthia fasciata – Zebra plant
Haworthia reinwardtii hybrid
Sedum rupestre 'Angelina'
Faucaria tigrina – Tiger jaws
Senecio radicans glauca – String of
　　bananas
Aeonium arboreum atropurpureum
　　'Zwartkop' –
　　Black tree aeonium
Portulacaria afra 'Variegata' –
　　Variegated elephant bush

SUPPLIES
Planting box or wagon with
　　drainage holes
Aquarium gravel
Glass pebbles
Sand
Craft paint
Miniature figurines
Cacti and succulent soil

5 SIMPLE HOW-TO STEPS TO CREATE
AFRICAN SAFARI GARDEN

1 Select a container that suits your desired size and space. Get creative and use a child's toy such as a Radio Flyer wagon or an oversized toy dump truck. Use anything the youngsters are willing to plant up.

2 Make sure to add drainage holes to the container of choice.

3 Select hardy "miniature" succulents and thornless cacti that resemble grass, trees, and bushes. This is the fun part!

4 Allow the kids to get involved in the selection process and read the labels aloud. Many succulents come from around the world, particularly Africa, and it can open a discussion about African animals and their habitat.

5 Layout the safari-themed garden—add gravel paths, riverbeds, and tall trees for the giraffe to nibble nearby. An easy way to control the placement of sand and gravel is by filling a plastic zipper-top bag, then cutting the tip of one corner; now, gently pour where desired.

DESIGNER NOTES
◆ **Trim any overgrown or leggy foliage that overtakes the miniature scale plantings,** and you and the kids can have another mini safari adventure to explore over and over again.

KID'S LIVING CHALKBOARD PLANTING

Why should teachers have all the fun? Writing with chalk is a blast! Getting students in school to participate makes classes more enjoyable for teachers and students alike. Here is an at-home activity that allows you to energize a mundane learning situation by combining conventional instruction with a unique, yet simple, chalkboard project.

A great way to approach the project as a learning tool is to plant a chosen succulent first and allow the plant to stimulate the child's imagination and creativity. It is especially inspiring to choose succulents with common names like tiger jaws, rattlesnake plant, elephant food, or crocodile plant.

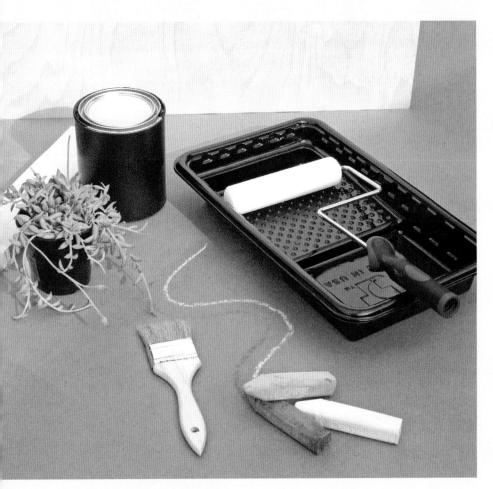

PLANTS

Sunflowers
Fenestraria aurantiaca – Baby toes

Monkey
Senecio radicans glauca –
    String of bananas
Aeonium decorum 'Sunburst'

Aloe-Gator
Aloe distans – Gold-tooth aloe
Kalanchoe eriophylla

SUPPLIES

Smooth wooden boards
Preassembled wood planter box
Latex primer
Paint rollers and trays
Chalkboard paint
L-brackets
Wood screws
Picture mounting kit
Heavy layer waterproof sheeting
Colored chalk
Matte finish sealant (optional)

KID'S LIVING CHALKBOARD PLANTING

1 Start with a clean, smooth board cut to your specifications, or use an existing chalkboard.

2 Wipe and clean the board so it is free of any loose debris. Sand completely smooth.

3 Apply a generous coat of latex primer. Allow to dry completely (follow directions on can).

4 Use a smooth finish roller to apply the first layer of chalkboard paint; allow to dry. Chalkboard paint may take up to 24 hours to dry between coat applications.

3

4a

4b

6

5 Apply a second coat of chalkboard paint. Repeat if necessary to thoroughly cover the board; allow to dry.

6 Assemble or purchase a preassembled wood planter box, and paint it with chalkboard paint as well.

7 Attach the planter box to the chalkboard with small L-brackets and ¼-in. wood screws.

7a

7b

8 There are two options: plant the selected succulents first and allow the plants to inspire the youngster's masterpiece, or draw an image and adapt the planting scheme right onto the board. Chalkboards allow for creative drawings and even educational labels to be added. Why not write the botanical name of the plants on the board for the kids to identify?

DESIGNER NOTES

◆ Combining chalkboards and succulent plants allows the kids to play and have fun while seizing an opportunity to teach or simply get them interested in horticulture at a young age. After writing the plant's botanical name on the chalkboard, **let the kids draw it into an image.** It is guaranteed that adults and children alike will enjoy making this masterpiece!

◆ **Keep the selected plants in their grower pots** so they may be easily removed for watering without smearing the work of art. This is especially important if the chalkboard is indoors.

◆ **If planting directly into a wood box, line the planter with sheeting** or seal with a waterproof coating.

◆ **To preserve the chalk art, simply spray the entire surface with a matte clear coat varnish.** These varnishes are readily found at craft and home-improvement stores.

8a

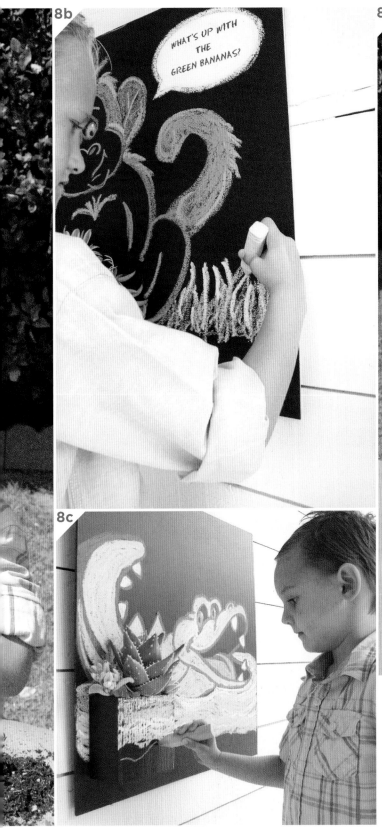

BACK-TO-NATURE PROJECTS

It is economical, exciting, creative, and most of all it just feels good to "repurpose" something rather than relegating the no-longer-used item to be a dark denizen of a closet, attic, garage, or worse, trash can. For a "can do" and "can up" simple and easy project, use empty tins as succulent containers, and should the lightning bolt of inspiration strike, go one step beyond by planting up a wooden pallet as an eye-candy backdrop showcasing the decorated cans.

For a conversation centerpiece, make a display of rocks with living stones, unique succulents that "mimic" the real things. Known as mimicry plants, they have uniquely adapted to their native desert habitats. In order to keep thirsty animals from browsing on their succulent leaves, these special plants have blended into the stark landscape by resembling rocks or gravel. When in place, marvel at how these "stone faces" resemble rocks, and when they bloom, there is the extra treat of vivid-colored, delicately beautiful flowers.

Another project transforms an old kitchen pot rack into a glittering chandelier "dripping" with succulents instead of crystal. And an empty wine bottle is no longer a sad reminder that the party is over. Nor should a special keepsake wedding champagne bottle or other special event stay tucked away in a cabinet. Bring empty bottles out to be remembered and admired by turning them into a "dry" bottle garden. There is even a "corking" idea for those wine corks packed away in the kitchen drawer!

CAN UP TIN CANS

Before 1957, tin cans were composed of tin and tinplate steel. Tin had important anti-corrosive properties and tinplate steel was not only low in price, but it added necessary strength to the container. From 1957 onward, aluminum became the metal of choice for "tin" cans. It is estimated that each person drinks one can of soda per day, but only 50 percent of those cans are recycled. Plus food, oil, and other types of cans are not included in this statistic. Here is a fun idea to up the ante on recycling cans, using them as succulent containers for interesting, textural, and attractive displays.

PLANTS
Aeonium arboreum 'Zwartkop'
Crassula rupestris 'Baby Necklace'
Echeveria elegans
Echeveria 'Crimson Tide' PPA

SUPPLIES
Cactus potting mix
Assorted tin cans
Craft spray paint
Metal drill bit and drill tool

A PALLET GARDEN

There are about a half a billion pallets made each year to carry and support goods for shipment. While they may be made out of a variety of materials, the most common is made of wood and most can support over 2,000 pounds. The renowned American acoustic guitar company Taylor Guitars constructed a "pallet guitar" out of pallet wood, not only to prove that construction technique was more important than pricey, exotic woods, but also because it was fun to make a quality guitar out of nontraditional materials. Our project is another example of using a pallet for a different, but stunning purpose.

Echeveria 'Blue Frills'
Aloe 'Crosby's Prolific'
Sedum mat (assorted sedums planted on a mat)

(Row 4, top to bottom)
Aeonium 'Zwartkop'
Echeveria elegans – Mexican snowball
Sedum mat (assorted sedums planted on a mat)
Echeveria 'Blue Frills'
Crassula perforata – String of buttons
Echeveria 'Tsunami'
Pachyveria 'Scheideckeri' – Jeweled crown
Sedum mat (assorted sedums planted on a mat)
Echeveria agavoides 'Martin's Hybrid'
Kalanchoe 'Satin Bells'

(Row 5, top to bottom)
Aeonium 'Zwartkop'
Kalanchoe 'Satin Bells'
Echeveria hybrid
Sedum mat (assorted sedums planted on a mat)
Sedum furfuraceum
Aloe 'Crosbys Prolific'
Echeveria 'Azulita'
Echeveria 'Crimson Tide'
Echeveria 'Gorgon's Grotto'
Senecio radicans glauca – String of bananas
Senecio scaposus – Silver coral
Echeveria hybrid

PLANTS

(Row 1, top to bottom)
Echeveria 'Perle Von Nurnberg'
Echeveria 'Blue Frills'
Sempervivum hybrid
Portulacaria afra – Elephant bush
Sedum mat (assorted sedums planted on a mat)
Oscularia deltoides – Pink ice plant
Echeveria 'Cass' Hybrid
Senecio mandraliscae – Blue chalk sticks
Crassula 'Baby Necklace'

(Row 2, top to bottom)
Echeveria 'Perle von Nurnberg'
Sedum mat (assorted sedums planted on a mat)
Echeveria 'Kirov'
Aeonium arboreum atropurpureum 'Zwartkop'
Kalanchoe longiflora coccinea
Echeveria 'Perle von Nurnberg'
Senecio mandraliscae – Blue chalk sticks

(Row 3, top to bottom)
Aeonium percarneum 'Kiwi'
Kalanchoe 'Teddy Bear'
Crassula 'Baby Necklace'

SUPPLIES
Wood pallet
Wood sealant
Weed barrier sheeting on a roll
Staple gun with staples
Hammer
Nails
Cactus potting mix
Plywood
Optional: wood stain

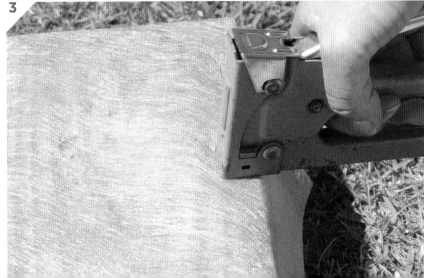

6 SIMPLE HOW-TO STEPS TO CREATE
A PALLET GARDEN

1 Start by cleaning the wood pallet. Once it is clean and dry, add a stain (if you like) and a clear wood sealant. Allow to dry thoroughly.

2 Measure a piece of weed barrier sheeting large enough to cover the back and sides of the pallet.

3 Using a staple gun, staple the weed barrier sheeting to the back of the pallet as tightly as possible.

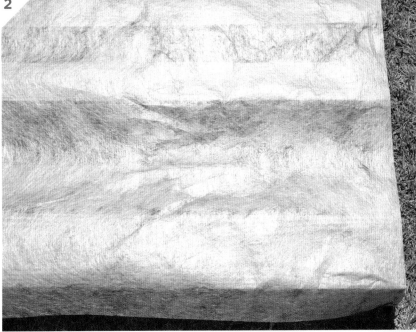

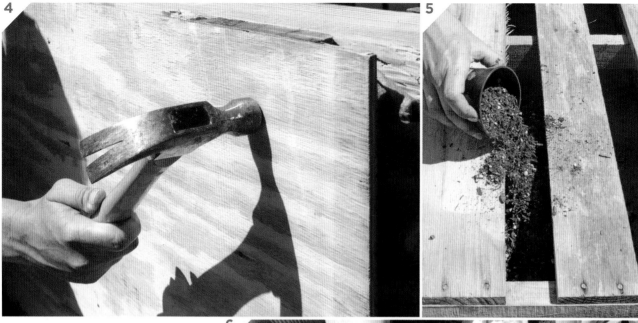

4 Position the pallet up, exposing the back and nail a piece of plywood to the back for added strength and support.

5 Turn the pallet over and fill it with cactus potting soil.

6 Plant the varieties of cactus and succulents, using various sizes and shapes to add interest and depth to the design.

DESIGNER NOTES
◆ **If you planted the pallet using cuttings or spaced plants loosely**, wait a couple weeks for them to root in firmly before standing the pallet up.
◆ **A pallet on its own is already relatively heavy**, but adding soil, succulents, and water makes it excessively heavy. Use caution when lifting and add very sturdy mechanics if you're hanging it on a wall. It might be a good idea to use a half pallet as shown in the accompanying photo. Or, enlist a friend to help you position the pallet vertically.

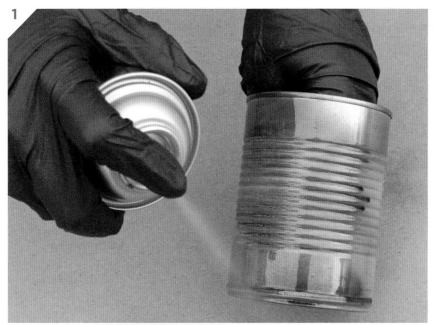

3 SIMPLE HOW-TO STEPS TO CREATE
CAN UP TIN CANS

1 Clean tin cans of various sizes. It is best to use a can opener leaving a finished edge rather than a jagged one. Paint the tin cans with craft spray paint. To antique, layer silver metallic, moss green, and wood stain spray paints, but make sure not to completely cover any one layer.

2 Drill a drainage hole in the bottom using a drill bit.

3 Fill with cactus potting mix, plant, and mount on a wall or nest together on the table as a multi-leveled centerpiece.

DESIGNER NOTES
◆ **This is also a great project to create with children.** Have them paint the cans in bright colors of their choosing and allow them to plant.
◆ **Recycled tin cans can also be wrapped in decorative scrapbook papers** and trims to suit any kind of party décor. Long term, the papers will not hold up when the plants are watered or exposed to the elements of weather.
◆ There are various ways to **hang your cans**, but the easiest is to drill a wood screw right through the upper back center of the tin can and secure it right to the wood.

LIVING STONES

Think of the desert landscape with its vast ripples of sand and dunes, broken up only by protruding rocks or washes of pebbles. How does a plant survive under such harsh conditions, and what can it do to camouflage itself with so much expansive, seemingly endless space, empty except for millions of rocks and gravel? The answer is to become like a rock, mimicking it so that browsing animals cannot find it or eat it. The fun of this project is to create an arrangement of "living stones" in combination with real stones or decorative rocks to trick any discerning eye.

PLANTS

Lithops – Stone faces
Pleiospilos nelii 'Royal Flush'
Sempervivum 'Pacific Devil's Food'
Senecio rowleyanus – String of pearls

SUPPLIES

Low, shallow container with drainage holes
Horticultural sand (available at garden centers and building supply stores; do *not* use beach sand)
River rocks (optional)

DESIGNER NOTES

- **Combine actual river rocks** with *Pleiospilos*, *Lithops*, and other mimicry succulents for a living puzzle.
- **A simple soil topper** such as horticultural sand (not beach sand because it is not sterile and has too much salinity) finishes the natural, sleek look and helps keep the arrangement dry.
- **Use the photo** as a design guide.

HANGING POT RACK CHANDELIER

There are always large, cumbersome items that were once useful and necessary in our day-to-day-lives, but which have become outdated or are no longer part of the design scheme. They are then relegated to the basement or other storage area, collecting dust and cobwebs. Such may be the case of the hanging pot rack. Perhaps it became more of a focus for clutter, or cooking with large heavy pots and pans that needed to be accessible was no longer part of our lifestyle. Whatever the reason, the following project is a beautiful way to repurpose this bulky item into a base for a succulent chandelier of magical proportions.

PLANTS
Crassula marginalis rubra variegata 'Calico Kitten'
Echeveria 'Magma'
Graptosedum 'California Sunset'
Opuntia subulata cristata
Senecio rowleyanus – String of pearls

SUPPLIES
Used or new pot rack
Moss or coco mat
Cactus potting mix
Candles, candleholders, hurricane glass cover and wooden round dowels,
    chopsticks or unsharpened pencils (optional)
Sturdy chain

HANGING POT RACK CHANDELIER

1 Line pot rack with a thick layer of moss or coco mat cut to the size and shape of the rack.

2 Add moss or coco mat to the sides, then fill with cactus potting mix to keep the walls and sides firm.

3 Plant with the selected varieties of cacti and succulents.

DESIGNER NOTES
◆ If adding candles, **provide supports under the candle dishes** so they are very stable. Long, round dowels work best and can be easily substituted with a wood chopstick or unsharpened pencil.
◆ For safety purposes, **use a hurricane glass** around the candle.
◆ **Hang with chain capable of supporting at least 100 lbs.**

1

2a

2b

DRY BOTTLE GARDENS

What can you do with all those empty bottles except to stick candles in them for alfresco dining, to make a bottle tree a la Martha Stewart, or to toss in the recycle bin? This project provides a much more creative way of using all those "99 bottles of beer on the wall" (or wine) for yourself and for friends. And to keep the bottle garden from rolling away, use those corks that have been moldering in the drawer to create an attractive and stable base. Besides the bottle, all that is needed is artistic imagination and the following "corking" good ideas!

PLANTS
Crassula dubia
Crassula 'Tom Thumb'
Jovibarba heuffelii
Crassula marginalis rubra variegata 'Calico Kitten'
Kalanchoe tomentosa – Teddy bear
Crassula perforata variegata
Senecio acaulis
Crassula argentea 'Gollum'
Crassula 'Mini Kitty'
Aloe
Crassula platyphylla
Pachyveria glauca 'Little Jewel'
Senecio scaposus
Crassula lycopodioides – Watch chain

SUPPLIES
Empty wine bottle or pre-cut wine bottles (see Resources)
Small rocks or gravel
Cactus potting mix or regular potting soil
Decorative river rock, moss, or sand
Dark horticultural sand (optional)

5 SIMPLE HOW-TO-STEPS TO CREATE
DRY BOTTLE GARDENS

1 Place your bottle garden on the stand (see instructions for bottle cork rest) or in a location that will not allow the rounded bottle to roll or shift.

2 Add small rock or gravel to the bottom for better drainage.

3 Add cactus soil mix.

4 Plant several small, slow-growing cacti and succulents. *Haworthia* and *Sempervium* species are good choices.

5 Finish with decorative river rock, moss, or sand.

DESIGNER NOTES
◆ **One major component of cactus and succulent soil is perlite,** but when used in a glass container, it may not be aesthetically pleasing even though perlite helps create well-draining soil that succulents require.
◆ An alternative is dark horticultural sand mixed into a potting soil without perlite.
◆ **The dark sand combined with the potting soil will disappear,** leaving a more refined and finished look, and it still creates good drainage.

WINE BOTTLE CORK REST

1 Take two wine corks, and drill two small pencil-lead-sized holes at each end, top and bottom.

2 Thread a thin, strong twine or string through the top hole of both wine corks and knot the string on the outer sides. Repeat through the bottom holes. The string between the corks should be no wider than your wine bottle (approx. 2 in.).

3 Once complete, it becomes a wine cork hammock/support to rest the wine bottle in and to keep it from tipping.

DESIGNER NOTES
◆ Cut recycled glass wine or liquor bottles as well as cork rests, such as the bottle garden photographed here, can be purchased online at http://bottle-gardens.com.
◆ Thin-coated leather twine is readily available at local craft and hobby stores usually in the jewelry making section. **The coated leather is easy to work with and very strong.**

SUPPLIES
2 wine corks
Drill
Strong twine, string, or leather twine

SEASONAL ARRANGEMENTS

Seasonal images are ordinarily thought of in terms of fresh sprigs of new growth, buds swelling and unfurling, fruits and berries emerging, heat-loving sunflowers following the sun, leaves burnished in reds, oranges, and yellows before drifting away, and the crystalline stillness of winter's frost outlining barren branches. Rarely are succulents regarded as a way to celebrate the four divisions of the year.

Because of their simple, elegant, and often colorful forms, succulents slip into many settings, especially as a divergence from the more mundane representations of the transitory seasons. With a bit of artistic license, succulents can serendipitously fill an empty cage with awakening warmth and color, while in summer they may evoke the refreshing coolness of a sea breeze. For autumn, succulents can mirror the burnished colors of autumn leaves, and in winter, they can replicate an outdoor winter wonderland with their foliage dusted in powdery whites.

The following projects are meant to inspire and to encourage the use of succulents so that their elegance and simplicity will celebrate any of the four seasons in an extraordinary fashion. Plus the results are long lasting with very little maintenance.

"SPRING" THE BIRD: CAGE THE SUCCULENTS
SUCCULENT BIRDCAGE

"Spring is the time of plans and projects."
—Leo Tolstoy, *Anna Karenina*

Spring is a time of awakening and renewal in the garden. In many parts of the country, it is also a beginning of outdoor activity. But wherever you are, the garden is waking up, and you're in control! Not only is gardening a fun way to play outdoors and get a little bit of exercise, but it is also the time to lay the foundation of visual delights for a new growing season.

Our birdcage project allows the activation of the gardening spirit that has too long been restricted by winter's elements. Use it as a simple garden ornament or a sophisticated natural design that begs for attention.

SPRINGTIME PROJECT PLANTS
Sempervivum species – Hens and chicks
Sempervivum arachnoideum 'Cebenese' – Cobweb houseleek
Echeveria gibbiflora v. *metallica* x *potosina*
Crassula arborescens subspecies *undulatifolia* 'Ripple Jade'
Echeveria agavoides
Kalanchoe delagoense variegata 'Pink Butterflies'
Sedum furfuraceum
Sempervivum hybrid 'Green'
Senecio radicans glauca 'String of Bananas'
Senecio jacobsenii
Echeveria hybrid 'Neon Breakers'
Echeveria 'Cass' hybrid
Sedum treleasei – Silver sedum

SUPPLIES
Birdcage
Coco mat
Cactus mix soil
Moss, ornamental feathers, and weed cloth (optional)

6 SIMPLE HOW-TO STEPS TO CREATE
"SPRING" THE BIRD

1 Start with any size birdcage. If it does not have a decorative rim at the top or a base to plant as shown here, simply apply the same simple steps for just the inside of the cage.

2 Lay down a foundation of coco mat or moss to create a planting area or "gutter" (planting trench) for the succulents.

3 Add a 2 in. foundation layer of cactus and succulent soil, just enough to start planting.

4 Remove some of the soil around the succulents, and gently position them in place.

5 Continue to plant, adding soil as needed.

6 Use moss or more coco matting around the edges to not only finish the cage, but also add a look fit for the makings of spring's loveliest nest. Add decorative feathers and accents if the spirit moves you.

DESIGNER NOTES

◆ If you're including live birds in the succulent-decorated cage, **select specimens that are nontoxic.** The toxicity depends on the plant itself, the size and species of the bird, and the amount ingested. Although many varieties of *Crassula* and *Aloe* are considered safe, it is important to confirm with your veterinarian to be positive. Add an extra layer of weed cloth as a barrier to prevent the birds from pulling apart and building a nest out of the coco matting.

◆ **Planting on top of birdcages requires more frequent watering** than your succulent container gardens because the soil is more exposed to air and will dry out faster than those planted in the soil.

◆ Finally, no artificial Styrofoam birds were harmed in this process.

SUMMERTIME: SOMEWHERE BEYOND THE SEA

"I'd give all the wealth that years have piled, the slow result of life's decay, to be once more a little child for one bright summer day."
—Lewis Carroll

Summer heat and humidity often encourage siestas rather than creativity, but while the garden grows and matures, remember that school is out. Children as well as adults can still enjoy a summer of fun and learning with garden craft projects that will keep them involved and outdoors in the garden all season long.

Everyone loves the beach in hot weather, and our summertime succulent projects are meant to reflect a seaside summer look. We love the combination of desert and nautical themes and summer may be the best season to purchase succulents from your local garden shop.

SUMMERTIME PROJECT PLANTS
Aloe distans
Senecio mandraliscae – Blue chalk sticks
Senecio rowleyanus – String of pearls
Sedum nussbaumerianum – Coppertone stonecrop
Aeonium 'Silver Edge'
Sedum spathulifolium 'Cape Blanco'
Echeveria 'Blue Sky'
Sempervivum calcareum

DESIGNER NOTES
- **The choice of plants and containers as pictured can be easily replicated or changed** depending on personal preferences. There really is no need for a set of how-to directions, making these projects especially fun!
- **If you don't live at the harbor, bring it to the patio!** Consider using sea glass (mosaic glass pieces), coral fans, seashells, horticultural sand (never beach sand), and any other marine accoutrement in your container gardens for a fresh sun-kissed, seaside summer look.
- **Use the same type of supplies** you see in the example photo; be creative!

FALLING FOR AUTUMN

"Delicious autumn! My very soul is wedded to it, and if I were a bird I would fly about the earth seeking the successive autumns."
—George Eliot

Autumn is one of the most interesting times of the year in the garden. Many parts of the country are preparing to hunker down for winter. Liberated from the need for an entire season of planning, gardeners can express a strong love for fall colors that mimic the changing scenery. While surrounding nature can be the underlying influence, practicality should dictate the season's projects. Our basket projects combine seasonal hues that make perfect centerpieces for any indoor or outdoor table setting.

FALL BASKET ARRANGEMENT
PLANTS
Aloe 'Rooikappie'
Senecio radicans glauca – String of bananas
Echeveria 'Lime & Chili'
Sedum rubrotinctum – Pork-n-beans
Euphorbia trigona 'Royal Red'– Good luck plant
Crassula capitella
Mammillaria elongata cristata 'Copper King'
Euphorbia tirucalli
Kalanchoe tomentosa 'Chocolate Soldier'
Sedum nussbaumerianum

LARGE ACCENT BASKET
WITH PERSIMMONS
PLANTS
Aloe nobilis – Gold-tooth aloe
Kalanchoe tomentosa 'Chocolate Soldier'
Crassula ovata 'Hummel's Sunset'

SUPPLIES
Cactus potting soil
Basket
Green sheet moss, chartreuse reindeer moss added to finish the arrangement with accents of French-wired natural jute ribbon and persimmons as display decor (optional)

DESIGNER NOTES
- **Use a very traditional fall color palette with a "pop" of brighter green to contrast the warm earthy tones** of cranberry, orange, and buttery yellow in dark wood baskets. The blooms of the *Aloe* 'Rooikappie' become the star, sharing vibrant height and vivid color.

LIGHT UP WINTER WHITE

"There is something infinitely healing in the repeated refrains of nature — the assurance that dawn comes after night, and spring after winter."
—Rachel Carson, *Silent Spring*

Succulents come in color palettes that adapt to any season of the year. Silvery whites, frosty blues, and pewter grays are the perfect tones for anyone anxious to do a little gardening even in the middle of winter. The textures, colors, and beauty of succulents are the basic elements for holiday arrangements.

WINTER WHITES
PLANTS
Aloe 'Blizzard'
Senecio scaposus – Silver coral
Cactus – Angel wings
Dudleya farinosa 'Chalk Rose'
Opuntia micodasys 'Albata'
Echeveria 'Cameo'
Echeveria 'Peacockii'
Kalanchoe hildebrandtii
Mammillaria fragilis – Thimble cactus
Lemaireocereus marginatus – Mexican fence post
Opuntia cylindrica cristata 'Emerald Idol'
Adromischus cristatus 'Key Lime Pie'

DESIGNER NOTES
◆ Some succulents naturally have a powdery "snow-dusted" finish to their leaves, so it's very easy to pull off a gorgeous, frosty winter centerpiece with minimal effort.
◆ The combination of icy blue and soft, powdery succulents, white spined cacti, and some interesting variegated aloes create a frosty winter showstopper that will last for seasons to come.
◆ For a touch of dazzle, try adding some crystal-flocked branches, artificial icicles, or clear crystal beads. To mimic this look, you can even glue crystals right onto branches found in your own backyard.
◆ Some glittering, container suggestions evocative of winter include silver mercury glass, white high gloss porcelain, or ceramic and mirrored metallics.
◆ For a dramatic, but budget-conscious arrangement on the buffet or bar, make an ice bowl and layer succulents inside on a bed of glass pebbles.
◆ If the container lacks a drainage hole, plant the succulents into a grower pot that fits inside the container, then remove the inner grower pot for easy watering. This will also protect any table's surface that is used for the centerpiece.

I do not literally paint that table,
But the emotion it produces upon me.

—Henri Matisse

OUTDOOR DÉCOR PROJECTS

Saucer projects are quick, easy ways to make design statements with a minimal amount of time and effort. The end result can be a satisfying creation for the novice or the experienced designer. How-to directions are often counterproductive to the creative musing needed for saucer projects, so engage the imagination and rev up the passion for results that are sure to reflect a personal design style. Use the following two saucer designs as inspiration, but don't be afraid to venture into a different look as long as the scale of the plants and the saucer are in proportion to each other.

A more advanced project, the living table arrangement more than compensates for the extra time and effort with plenty of oohs and aahs. Here are both an economical option and one for the designer afflicted with "succulent fever" who cries out, "Look at me!"

The list of suggested succulent plants is merely a guideline, so whether selecting specimens for the saucer or table projects, give free reign to personal preferences, but again, keep in mind that size and appropriate scale should be considered.

LOW CLAY SAUCERS

While saucers are designed to hold water that drains from potted plants, they can also make excellent containers for shallow-rooted succulents. Clay or ceramic saucers can be purchased in a variety of colors and shapes that complement the assortment of succulents being displayed. Rosette-shaped echeverias often show their best features in low-profile planters.

Though the container doesn't need to be deep, drainage is important. Plants will require less care if a power drill and masonry bit is used to drill several small drainage holes in the bottom of the saucer. It's a good idea to paint the inside surface of low-fired clay containers with a sealant to prevent deterioration.

AQUA/TURQUOISE SAUCER PLANTS

Kalanchoe panamensis
Echeveria hybrid 'Neon Breakers'
Pleiospilos nelii 'Royal Flush' – Split rocks

Crassula 'Jade Necklace'
  (*C. falcata* x *C. marnieriana*)
Fenestraria aurantiaca 'Baby Toes'

SUPPLIES
Cactus potting soil
Green reindeer moss
Green iridescent marbles

DARK GREEN SAUCER
PLANTS
Echeveria hybrid 'Set-Oliver'
Aloe hariana 'Mosaic Aloe'
Echeveria affinis 'Black Knight'
Senecio rowleyanus –
  String of pearls
Sempervivum arachnoideum v.
  'Cebenese' – Cobweb houseleek
Euphorbia lactea cristata variegata – Alabaster swirl
Crassula conjuncta
Euphorbia flanaganii cristata – Green coral

SUPPLIES
Cactus potting soil
Sheet moss (added as a soil topper)
Glass votive candles with chartreuse tea light candles

1 SIMPLE HOW-TO STEP TO CREATE
LOW CLAY SAUCERS

1 Select a saucer that suits one's design sensibility and either follow the photo examples or veer off into a different direction.

DESIGN NOTES
◆ **Remember, if using a clay saucer, to purchase one with a glazed interior** or paint the interior with a clay sealant to prevent staining of finished surfaces.

A LIVING SUCCULENT TABLE

We have seen tables incorporating living succulents sell for well over $1,000. Since our imaginations are not as limited as our budgets, we felt that there must be a practical, yet sophisticated way for anyone to fabricate a similar piece.

Our crackerjack designer Robyn has come up with two ways to create this lovely conversation piece. The first motif is accomplished with the frugal purchase of a table from IKEA, and the second involves retrofitting an existing table. Either method results in a precious, useable, yet inexpensive piece of succulent furniture. Perhaps our plan will provide inspiration for other succulent furnishings.

TABLE 1 PLANTS (RIGHT TO LEFT)
Adromischus cristatus
Echeveria 'Azulita'
Graptosedum 'Alpenglow'
Sedum mat (an assortment of mixed Sedum grown on a mat)
Echeveria pulidonis
Crassula rupestris 'Baby Necklace'
Echeveria 'Perle Von Nurnberg'
Echeveria 'Topsy Turvy'
Sedum lucidum cristata

TABLE 1 SUPPLIES
Assembly-required new table
Green sheet moss
Cactus potting soil
Screening material

7 SIMPLE HOW-TO STEPS TO CREATE
A LIVING SUCCULENT TABLE

1 This table was purchased at IKEA, and assembly was required. During the assembly process of this simple table with shelf and glass top, flip over the shelf portion and assemble it upside down to create a "tray" rather than a shelf. This will allow for a depth of 2 in. to plant the succulents.

2 A liner is necessary to hold the soil and plants while still allowing for drainage. Although a natural fiber coco mat or greenhouse shade cloth will work fine, window screening is the easiest, providing both durability and excellent drainage. Cut the screening about 2 in. wider and longer than the tray.

3 Add cactus soil on top of the screening.

4 Pack in the soil, and trim off any excess screen to make the edges and corners nice and neat.

5 Now it is time to plant! Because the tray is only 4 in. from the top of the table (when the glass is in place), it is best to choose smaller 2-in. plants or cuttings.

6 Depending on design preference, use moss to finish any areas showing soil, but keep in mind that many varieties will spread and quickly fill the spaces.

7 Place the glass on top, and voila! It's time to enjoy a living table.

A LIVING SUCCULENT TABLE
OPTION 2

PLANTS
Echeveria 'Perle Von Nurnberg'
Echeveria 'Princess Blue'
Echeveria 'Tippy'
Echeveria harmsii – Plush plant
Echeveria agavoides 'Red Tip'
Echeveria 'Aquarius'
Echeveria imbricata – Blue rose
Echeveria 'Neon Breakers'
Aeonium 'Irish Bouquet'
Sedum rubrotinctum 'Aurora'
Senecio radicans glauca

SUPPLIES
Existing table
Cactus potting soil
Green sheet moss
River rock
Horticultural sand
3 sturdy glass candlestick or votive candleholders
   or juice glasses
Glass top to fit your existing table

7 SIMPLE HOW-TO STEPS TO CREATE
A LIVING SUCCULENT
TABLE, OPTION 2

1 Protect the table and any linen covering with a layer of heavy-duty plastic sheeting or weed cloth cut to size.

2 Position the support juice glasses, candlestick, or votive candleholders in a triangle-shape on the table so the top glass will have enough support to be steady and level. You may need to add the glass top, position it to make sure, and then remove the glass for decorating.

3 Pile on a thin layer of soil as if you were planting a garden bed.

4 Remove plants from packs or containers and pull away some of the soil, leaving the root ball. Place the succulents all around the table surface.

5 Add "paths" of river rock and patches of sand to fill in other areas.

6 Finish off all edges and any exposed soil with moss. Be creative and add personal touches.

7 Add the glass top, and you're ready to enjoy a living table!

DESIGNER NOTES
◆ **Do *not* overwater;** succulents thrive in drier soil. Once every other week should be more than enough. Add fertilizer formulated for succulents about once a month to keep plants healthy.
◆ **The best location is a patio or deck with morning sun** exposure because succulents love light and need gentle sun, but not too much or they may burn.
◆ **Table 2 is ideal for a special event or party as a service table.** With the added plants and glass top, the increased height makes the tabletop too tall to sit at, but it is perfect for table service such as a wine station or hors d'oeuvres.
◆ **For a party, Table 1 or 2 can be prepared in advance** so that it is ready to go for the perfect show-stopping accent without the stress of a last-minute project. Just set it out and enjoy the compliments.

BASICS OF SUCCULENT CARE

Succulents are rapidly growing in popularity for two simple reasons: they are bewitchingly beautiful and genuinely easy to care for. The water-storing adaptations of stems, leaves, roots, and trunks that form the incredible shapes of these plants also work to develop plants that are survivors and require little care. However, while minimal care is required to maintain magnificent succulents, this culture can be exact and unforgiving.

Following these general rules should provide the gardener with plants that are healthy and impressive. They basically involve guidelines that not only re-create a succulent habitat, but also improve upon it. Succulents in the wild often look like they are barely surviving, but when coddled in captivity, they really are more impressive.

WATERING BASICS, OR DON'T LET ME DIE IN THIS SWAMP!

It is likely not too much of a stretch to say that problems with moisture and light are responsible for virtually all deaths of succulent plants in the home or garden. The roots of succulents are designed to take up water very quickly and efficiently. While this attribute adapts them very well to arid, desert-like conditions, the tradeoff is that these plants do not have the capacity to swiftly get rid of excess water in quagmire conditions. Overwatering, especially combined with cool temperatures, induces rotting of plant tissues, and the succulent becomes a mushy mess. This potential for rot is one justification for the importance of fast-draining soils or cactus mixes when potting succulents.

On the other hand, it is important to debunk the myth that succulents never require much water. In their habitats, small desert plants may have roots pervading an area that is quite in excess of the diameter of the plant. In the absence of rainfall, these extended root systems can utilize heavy dews or mists. In containers,

Damage from overwatering

the plants do not have access to this natural source of moisture, so it must be supplied. Assuming plants are getting the proper amount of light and are in a proper medium, succulents should never receive just sprinkles of water. Pots should be thoroughly watered until water runs out the drainage hole in the bottom of the container. A lack of water will cause roots to desiccate and die. Since dried roots cannot take up water, plants become prone to rotting.

Once a succulent has been well watered and any excess has been removed from the saucer, the question of when to water next can be perplexing. Some people use this handy tip. Place a flat stone on the surface of the soil, near the plant. If there is still moisture under the stone when it is lifted, do not water. If the area is completely dry, it is time to water again. Most succulent growers use this general rule of thumb: "If you are not sure whether to water a succulent, don't." Most cacti and other succulents have an active growing period in spring and summer. Once the weather has warmed, it is usually time to begin regular watering.

LIGHT REQUIREMENTS, OR HOW MANY PLANTS GROW IN CAVES?

While intense, direct sunlight combined with hot temperatures is a situation that most succulents can survive, it is not one in which they will thrive. Indoor lighting conditions are often cave-like, so south-facing windows are important for winter survival. However, when grown outdoors, succulents look best when protected from the scorching rays of the sun. Light intensity is especially important if you are moving plants from indoors to outdoors.

Most people would never think of going directly from Minnesota to a Hawaiian beach in January without plenty of sunscreen. Plants can also sunburn. Plant leaves are covered with a waxy layer called a cuticle that thickens to prevent burning, just as a tan protects human skin. Indoors, this cuticle thins out to allow in as much light as possible. Moving a

Sun damage

plant directly outdoors is akin to going to the beach without sunscreen, and permanent scarring can occur, especially on cacti. Plants can be acclimated to a drastic change by placing them in filtered light, then moving them gradually to higher light conditions.

Light is paramount to healthy succulent growth. If succulents, especially cacti, are receiving too little light, they may produce etiolated growth. Etiolation is a process that occurs in plants grown in partial or the complete absence of light. It is typified by long, weak stems; smaller, sparser leaves due to longer internodes; and chlorosis. In most cases, it is natural for a plant to grow toward a light source, but it is crucial to avoid extreme reaching. A columnar cactus that is bent toward the window at a 90-degree angle is not a pretty sight.

TEMPERATURE, OR TODAY ON SURVIVOR

Temperature is an important factor to the health of cacti and succulents. On the whole, they are more cold tolerant than is generally assumed. However, the water-storing capacity of the cells also provides the opportunity for those cells to burst under freezing conditions, resulting in a slushy mess of a plant. In the desert, there is often a marked contrast between night and daytime temperatures. Most succulents thrive in colder nights, as long as the thermometer does not dip below freezing. Optimally, these plants prefer daytime temperatures between 70°F and 85°F and nighttime temperatures between 50°F and 55°F.

When growing plants indoors, a drop in temperature can often result in the initiation of flower buds. Areas right next to windows often provide the ideal temperature differential during the winter and can satisfy the cool temperatures needed to trigger flowering. While normal room temperatures will not harm the plants, they may be prevented from blooming. This is especially true of many cacti, especially those that are globe-shaped, which are for more apt to bloom if given a cool, dry period.

Hardy succulent plants can bring beauty, versatility, and interest to perennial gardens, even to USDA Hardiness Zone 3. Beal Gardens on the campus of Michigan State University in East Lansing has had survivor opuntia cacti growing happily (or at least reluctantly) for over 50 years. There are even websites specializing in the sale of hardier succulent plants, so if you're growing succulents in colder climates, be

Frost damage

creative and substitute some of those choices in the project designs presented here.

POTTING SOILS, OR DIRT IS DEAD, SOIL IS ALIVE!

Light and temperature are often difficult to control, but the type of medium that succulents are planted into is well within every gardener's control. If purchasing a commercial soil, it should be a fast-draining mixture that is specifically designed for cacti and succulents. If one is not readily available, it is simple to modify all-purpose potting mixes with fast-draining amendments like perlite to increase aeration and drainage. Succulents generally have shallow roots that form a dense mat just under the soil surface, and this area needs to dry out quickly.

Since the native soils of succulent plants are usually not high in nutrients, organic material is not as important to their well-being, but sterilized mixes should still be avoided. Soils rich in soil microbes are healthier for all plant life. To create a suitable succulent soil mix, use two parts by volume of a potting mix (preferably one that is not peat-based), one part perlite, and one part small-sized gravel like pumice. If the gravel is not handy, a 1:1 mixture of potting soil and perlite will do just as well. A speedy exchange between water and air is vital in the root zone of succulent plants; a soil that remains wet for long periods of time will signal the demise of most succulent plants.

FERTILIZER NEEDS, OR MOM SAYS I'M NOT FAT, I'M JUST PLUMP

Everyone knows that succulents need to store water because of the arid conditions that are typical of their environments. Less realized is the fact that this water-storing ability also allows for the storage of food. Food plus water retention equals plump plants; excess food plus excess water adds up to morbidly obese plants that are sickly if they survive at all. Succulents, like teenagers, can have a rabid appetite when actively growing, and during this period, they can be fed with a balanced (one that has roughly equal proportions of nitrogen, phosphorous, and potassium) plant food. Follow the directions on the label, but only use half of the amount that is recommended for other plants.

As autumn approaches and the weather begins to cool, daylight hours shorten and succulent plants enter their nonactive rest period. Plants should not be fertilized during this stage of dormancy. Some succulents are winter active, in which case the theory still holds, but the timing is modified. Remember, succulents that look fat and happy are usually doing just fine and the parental urge to feed them should be resisted.

Mealybugs

BASICS OF SUCCULENT PEST PROBLEMS

Undoubtedly cacti and succulents are rugged, resilient, and all-around tough plants. However, they are still susceptible to invaders from the animal kingdom that view them as nothing more than a "succulent" feast. Water-rich cells also contain nutrients that are compelling to both sucking and chewing pests. Mealy bugs, aphids, slugs, and scale insects are among some of the bugs that can create havoc in a succulent collection. Insect problems are notably difficult to control, since pesticides containing oils can damage the surface of many cacti and succulents. It is also important to note that sprays containing malathion will damage or kill many plants in the *Crassulaceae* family, which includes Aeonium, Echeveria, Sedum, and Jade plants.

MEALYBUGS

It seems that virtually no assemblage of succulents survives for long without an attack from mealybugs. They are tiny insects about one-tenth of an inch in length that wrap themselves in a cottony, protective coating. Mealybugs live their entire adult lives within their cottony garrisons, blissfully consuming plant sap. Plants infested with these insects grow more slowly, become weaker, and may become susceptible to

diseases. As if these cottony masses were not annoying enough, there are also mealybugs that attack the roots of succulents. Whether above or below the soil, they are protected from both predators and pesticides by their cottony coverings. Minor infestations can be managed by wiping the visible masses with a cotton swab that has been dipped in rubbing alcohol. The alcohol dissolves the insulating covering, but followup applications need to be made in order to ensure complete control. Systemic insecticides that are applied to the soil may be effective in many instances as long as they are applied during the growing season when the plant is actively taking up moisture from the soil.

SPIDER MITES

Spider mites are miniscule creatures that are barely visible without the aid of a magnifying glass. As their populations increase, webs can be seen covering the surface of the plant. They, too, are sap suckers, and infected succulents often develop yellowish spots that later become brownish, permanently scarring the plant. Plants that have been weakened by considerable sap quaffing become susceptible to subsequent bacterial or fungal diseases.

Since spider mites despise being wet, jets of water are usually advised as a cure for the problem. However, since succulent plants also detest being wet, care must be given to keeping the soil from becoming too soggy. Spider mites are not insects. They are, well, mites, and so most insecticides are ineffective in their control. Serious problems require the use of a miticide.

Aloe mite damage

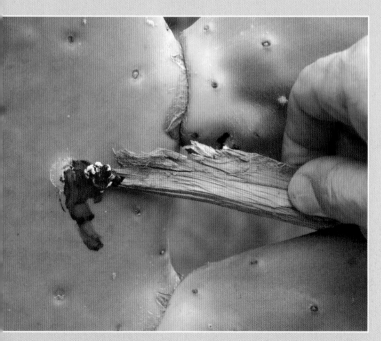
Cochineal scale

SCALE INSECTS

Although Wikipedia claims there are over 8,000 species of scale insects, the ones most likely to be found on succulents are armored scales. The moniker comes from the scale-like bomb shelters that these pests hide under. The insects multiply quickly and left untreated will rapidly cover the surface of a succulent. Scales prefer shade and are usually found on the shady sides of plants. Control of scale is the same as it is for mealybugs.

SLUGS AND SNAILS

These are only a problem outdoors, but under ideal conditions, they spread rapidly and attack the softer new growth of cacti and succulents. They are perversely fond of flower buds. Fortunately, these gastropods can be organically controlled with snail and slug bait products that contain iron phosphate. They are safe to use around pets, humans, fish, birds, beneficial insects, and mammals. If the bait is not consumed by a slug or snail, the material breaks down into fertilizer.

Snail damage

BASICS OF SUCCULENT PROPAGATION

Like the "old woman who lived in a shoe,"
Most succulents propagate so easily that you won't know what to do.

Actually there are plenty of things to do with extra succulents, or we would not have written this book. Of course, there are many rare plants that are not cooperative and difficult to reproduce, but generally the process of making new plants is easy enough for the whole family to enjoy. Here are some of the simplest methods of propagation.

SEEDS

All cacti and succulents are flowering plants, so in theory, they should all be able to be propagated by seed. However, due to the tortoise-like growth of some species, other techniques are more practical. Cactus and succulent seeds are available from many online seed companies or can be collected from plants in the landscape, as fresh seed may germinate more readily than seed from other sources.

5 SIMPLE STEPS FOR
GROWING FROM SEED

Start with clean pots or trays in which to sow the seed. If the trays have been used in the past, it is a good idea to disinfect them with a solution of 1 part bleach to 10 parts water. Since fast drainage is important, use shallow containers that are not deeper than about 4 in. Fill the trays with a mix that is equal parts potting soil and either perlite, sharp sand, or pumice. Most seeds can germinate well enough in plain sand (but not beach sand; it contains too much salt).

If metal containers are not being used, the planters made of sturdy nonmetal materials can be sterilized in a microwave. Microwave the soil for about 90 seconds on full power. Allow the soil mix to cool, and water it thoroughly. Let it drain but not dry out. Fill the propagation pans with the moist soil mixture to about ½ in. below the rim.

Most seeds will germinate best if sown in early spring. The seeds should be scattered over loose soil and then pressed in lightly. Covering the soil with a fine layer of sand to hold them in place is also helpful. Cover the seed trays with clear plastic wrap, and place them in a bright location but out of direct sunlight.

Many cacti and succulents will germinate within three weeks, but there are species that can require as much as a year to begin growing. When seedlings appear, remove the plastic wrap. The soil should not be allowed to dry out, but seedlings are fragile, so moisten them with very fine mists of water.

Once plants are about six months old, they can be transplanted into individual containers. As a general rule, cacti can be transplanted when they are the size of a large marble, and other succulents can be transplanted when they are about 3 in. tall. Gently lift the plants from the growing medium in the seed trays, set them into the soil of the new container, and water them in. Then topdress the pot with sand, gravel, or pumice.

STEM CUTTINGS

Propagation by stem cuttings is simple and practical. Since pruning shears can crush tissues, it is normally best to use a sharp razor blade or knife that has been sterilized with alcohol to remove a cutting from the parent plant. A clean cut allows the cutting to heal fast enough to persist without water during the callusing stage. During this period, the exposed cut of the succulent is allowed to form a protective callus. This process, which takes about a week, is best done in a warm, shady spot outdoors. Once the callus has formed, the cutting is less prone to rot and is ready to be placed in the rooting medium.

Plant the callused stem cutting into a cactus, sand, or perlite medium and water immediately. Then do not water until the soil begins to dry out. Taller cuttings may need to be staked until they root to keep them from falling over. After a few weeks, the succulent stems should have rooted enough to transfer them into a larger container. Do not overpot; keep the size of the planter proportionate to the size of the root system.

You can grow a whole new plant from a small cutting such as this.

LEAF CUTTINGS

Unlike most leafy plants, a wide range of succulents are very easily propagated by leaf cuttings. Just like stem cuttings, leaf cuttings are best taken at the beginning of the active growing season. This is a great project in which to involve children. The cutting and callusing process is similar to that of stem cutting as described above, but usually half the amount of time is required for the cut part to callus over. The cut tips should just barely be pushed into the soil where root formation will begin. The small leaves of many sedums are often just scattered over the tops of moistened sand in order to propagate them. Once a new plant has begun to form, the old leaf can be used as a handle to move the baby plant into its new pot.

After callusing, succulent cuttings are inserted into quick-draining cactus mix to form new plants.

Plantlets forming on the flowering stalk of an Agave can be gently removed and repotted.

Some of the groups of succulents that are easily propagated by leaf cuttings include but are not limited to the following:

> *Crassula*
> *Echeveria*
> *Gasteria*
> *Graptopetalum*
> *Haworthia*
> *Kalanchoe*
> *Sansevieria* (though variegated cultivars may lose their coloring)
> *Sedum*

PLANTLETS AND OFFSETS

A number of cacti and succulents form offsets or "babies" that develop around the mother plant. These newborns can be removed by gently twisting them away from the mother plant and repotted. If the offsets are close to the ground, they will have probably already put out a small root system and are ready to be repotted. Numerous succulents, notably sansevierias and agaves, spread by means of underground lateral shoots. As these shoots give rise to new plants, these can be severed from the main plant, callused, and replanted to produce an independent plant.

Several *Kalanchoe spp.* produce small plantlets often bearing juvenile roots on the edges of their leaves. These readily detach and are have an uncanny ability to create new starter succulents. Agave and furcraea plants grow for many years before finally flowering once and then dying. Often small plantlets will form on the old flower stalks that will readily root to become new plants. Here is a list of some cacti and succulent groups that can produce plantlets or offsets:

> *Agave*
> *Aloe*
> *Echinopsis*
> *Kalanchoe*
> *Mammillaria*
> *Sansevieria*

RESOURCES

Many wonderful succulents can be purchased from local garden on home improvement centers. There are also a number of reputable mail-order companies that specialize in harder-to-find and extra-hardy plants. We have chosen a few that have had good reputations for quality and dependability in past years. There are many good suppliers besides these, but always exercise caution when ordering from unfamiliar businesses.

COMPANY NAME	LOCATION	WEBSITE
Arid Lands Greenhouses	Tucson, AZ	www.aridlands.com
Bottle Gardens & More	San Diego, CA	www.bottle-gardens.com
Cactuslands	Tucson, CA	www.cactuslands.com
CactusStore	Phoenix, CA	www.cactusstore.com
Cold Hardy Cactus	Lakewood, CO	www.coldhardycactus.com
GardenLIfe	Vista, CA	www.gardenlife.com
Grigsby Cactus Garden	Vista, CA	www.cactus-mall.com/grigsby
Highland Succulents	Gallipolis, OH	www.highlandsucculents.com
Institute for Aloe Studies	Oakland, CA	www.aloestudies.org
Intermountain Cactus	Kaysville, UT	www.intermountaincactus.com
J&J Cactus and Succulents	Midwest City, OK	www.jjcactus-succulents.net
Jadepoint Succulents	Minot, ND	www.jadepoint.com
Living Stones Nursery	Tucson, AZ	www.lithops.net
North Hills Nursery	Rock Cave, WV	www.northhillsnursery.com
Rio Grande Cacti	Socorro, NM	www.riograndecacti.com
Simply Succulents Nursery	Cable, WI	www.simplysucculents.com

INDEX

MEET THE AUTHORS

JOHN BAGNASCO

John Bagnasco has been in the gardening industry for over forty-five years, starting with a degree in horticultural marketing, followed by a ten-year stint at Frank's Nursery and Crafts in Detroit. After 1976, he moved to California to become regional manager and buyer for the Nurseryland division of Sunbelt Nursery Group. He then became the head buyer for Armstrong Garden Centers based in Glendora, California. John is currently the president and co-host with Sharon Asakawa of the nationally syndicated GardenLife radio show, which reaches 1.1 million listeners every weekend. He is the president of www.GardenTube.com, a YouTube-type site for gardeners, and he is a partner in SuperNaturals Grafted Vegetables, LLC.

SHARON ASAKAWA

Bruce and Sharon Asakawa are legends in the plant world, especially in their home state of California. Bruce "grew up" in the nursery business, as his parents founded and operated a well-known garden center, which Bruce and Sharon ran. In addition to developing and teaching horticulture classes and becoming garden communicators with radio and television programs, Bruce and Sharon led garden tours around the world. Their books include Bruce and Sharon Asakawa's California Gardener's Guide, California Gardening Rhythms, California Gardener's Handbook, and the soon-to-be-published California Getting Started Garden Guide. You can catch up with Sharon weekly on the national gardening and lifestyle news talk radio program GardenLife, which airs every Saturday from 8-9 a.m. and Sunday from 8-10 p.m. PST. You can call in directly at 1-800-606-TALK with your garden questions. She'd love to hear from you.

SHAUN BUCHANAN

Shaun Buchanan is a professional User Experience designer, and has been designing and photographing for the last decade. As an in-house designer at a plant nursery in North County San Diego, where he currently resides with his wife Kate, he developed a love for cacti and succulents while photographing and designing ads for marketing material. This is his first book.

ROBYN FOREMAN

Robyn M. Foreman is a highly skilled and trained floral designer with more than twenty-five years experience. Her business specializes in custom upscale events with a focus on décor and outrageous florals. Nothing is off limits to use in her design work; if it's beautiful, alive and can't run away on its own its going in an arrangement! Cacti and succulents are a perfect medium to create some intriguing, lavish looks. Recently Robyn was featured in the Better Homes and Gardens special interest publication Country Gardens with her fresh take on combining flowers with succulents in everyday arrangements. This is her first book.